NAMED GIANTS. REAL BATTLES. ETERNAL VICTORY.

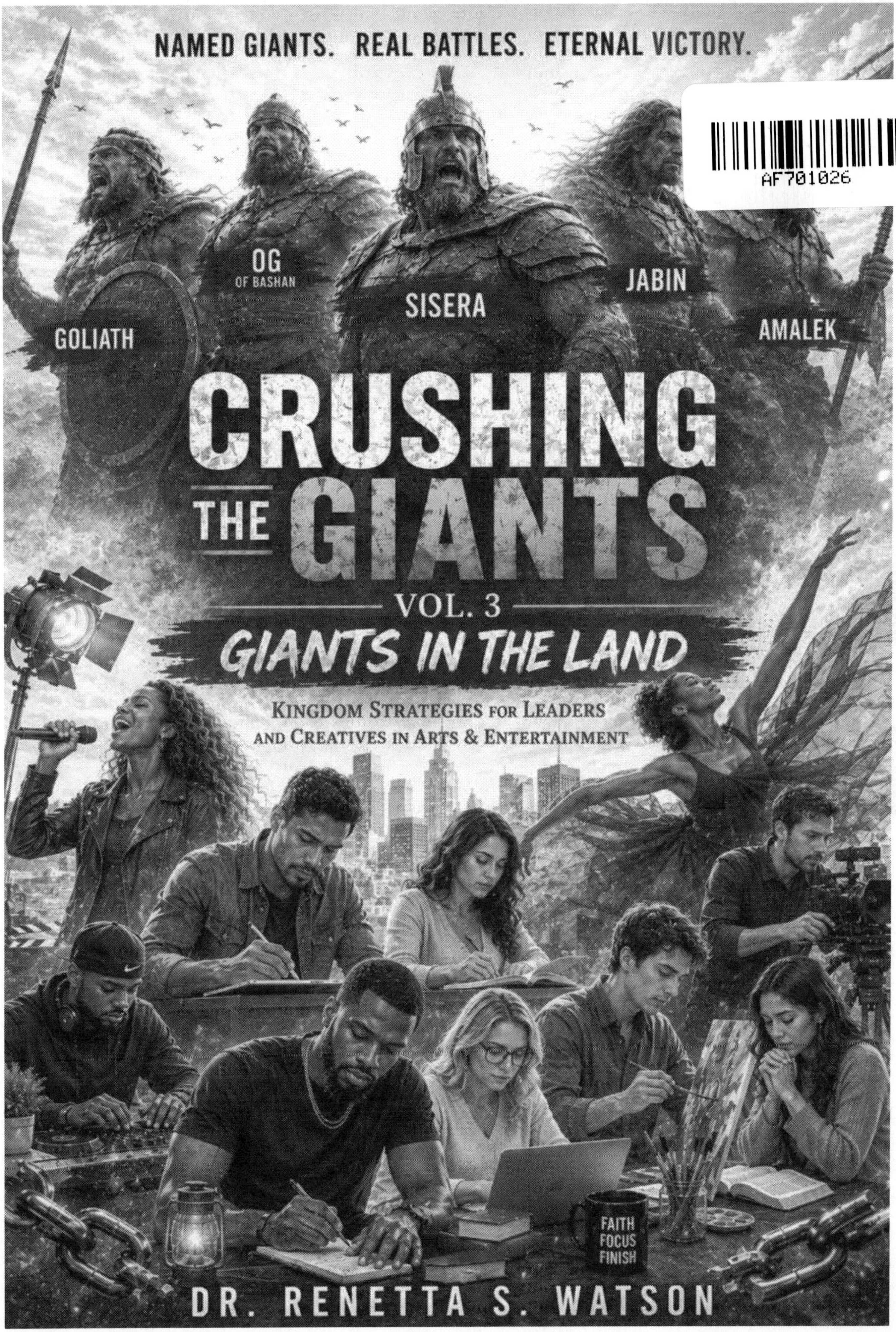

CRUSHING THE GIANTS

VOL. 3

GIANTS IN THE LAND

KINGDOM STRATEGIES FOR LEADERS AND CREATIVES IN ARTS & ENTERTAINMENT

DR. RENETTA S. WATSON

AF701026

CRUSHING THE GIANTS

KINGDOM STRATEGIES FOR CREATIVES IN ARTS AND ENTERTAINMENT

VOLUME 3 – GIANTS IN THE LAND

Dr. Renetta S Watson

The EQUIPPER

Giving you the tools to turn your Next into Now.

DrRenettaSWatson@yahoo.com
314-312-3448
RenettaSWatson.com
CrushingTheGiants.com

© 2026 E.D.U.K.A.T.E. Ministries

Published by
ACT Publishing
An imprint of A Caring Touch Design & Publishing

A CARING TOUCH
DESIGN & PUBLISHING
Impress · Impact · Inspire

TABLE OF CONTENTS

PREFACE

Up until this point, we have dealt with giants that are often formed within. These are the kinds of giants that develop internally, through experiences, wounds, mindsets, and mixture. They shape how we think, how we respond, how we see ourselves, and ultimately how we move.

And while we saw examples and patterns of these throughout Scripture, many of those giants were not always given specific names.

They were revealed through behaviors, patterns, responses, and spiritual conditions.

But now, we shift. In this volume, we move from internal formation to external confrontation. Here, we are going to deal with actual, named giants in the Bible. These are giants that lived in real places, ruled over territories, fought in physical battles, and stood between God's people and what God promised them.

These are not just symbolic. These are the giants that occupied the land. These are the giants that had to be faced, fought, and defeated. And what makes this powerful is this, every one of these giants is connected to a real war. Not theory. Not imagination. These were battles that actually happened. But they were never just natural battles. They were spiritual confrontations wrapped in physical warfare.

And what we are going to do in this volume is take a deeper look at them. We are going to explore their names, understand what their names mean, study where they lived, uncover why they existed, examine how they operated, and most importantly, learn how they were defeated.

Because these giants are not just history. They are patterns. You may not face a literal giant standing in front of you, but you will face intimidation, resistance, opposition, delay, pressure at new levels, battles tied to territory and assignment. And these biblical giants give us language, strategy, and insight into how to deal with what we face today.

THE 4 TYPES OF GIANTS

Before we deal with the giants, you must understand how they operate.

1. IDENTITY GIANTS (Must Be Defeated)

These attack who you believe you are. They don't start with your situation; they start with your self-perception.

Example: Numbers 13:33 "We were like grasshoppers in our own sight..."

What they do is shrink your confidence, distort your identity, and make you disqualify yourself.

How you win: You don't fight them physically; you replace lies with truth.

2. INTERNAL GIANTS (Must Be Dismantled)

These live inside of you, thought patterns, emotional wounds, and hidden struggles. What they do is sabotage progress, create cycles, and distort decision-making.

How you win: Through renewal, healing, and exposure.

3. STRONGHOLD / GENERATIONAL GIANTS (Must Be Displaced)

These are long-standing systems, family patterns, cultural cycles, and spiritual strongholds. What they do is repeat patterns, resist change, and sit on your inheritance.

How you win: You drive them out over time with consistency.

4. SEASONAL / STRATEGIC GIANTS (Must Be Navigated)

These giants show up at key moments, when you're tired, when you're, transitioning, and when you're close to breakthrough. What they do is test your timing and exploit your vulnerability.

How you win: Through discernment, timing, and endurance.

UNDERSTANDING HOW GIANTS MUST BE DEALT WITH

Not every giant is handled the same way. Some giants must be defeated and destroyed, while others must be dismantled.

Revelation: You must know what kind of giant you are facing so you know how to fight it.

Identity giants must be defeated. Internal giants must be dismantled. Stronghold / generational giants must be displaced. Seasonal / strategic giants must be navigated. If these are not understood correctly, people will win moments but lose territory, break cycles temporarily but not permanently, and get blindsided in new seasons. This is why each type of giant must be handled with the right strategy.

IDENTITY GIANTS MUST BE DEFEATED AND INTERNAL GIANTS MUST BE DISMANTLED

Identity giants must be defeated because they attack who you believe you are. They do not begin with your situation; they begin with your perception. If they can distort your identity, they can control your decisions.

Numbers 13:33 says, "We were like grasshoppers in our own sight…" Before the enemy ever defeated them externally, they were already defeated internally in how they saw themselves. That is why identity giants require defeat. They must be confronted directly with truth and overthrown. John 8:32 says, "Ye shall know the truth, and the truth shall make you free." When truth is applied, identity is restored, and the giant loses its power.

Internal giants must be dismantled because they are not standing in front of you; they are operating within you. These are thought patterns, emotional wounds, and hidden agreements that shape behavior and create cycles. You cannot simply cast these out or confront them externally because they are rooted internally.

Romans 12:2 says, "Be transformed by the renewing of your mind…" Second Corinthians 10:4–5 says, "…pulling down strongholds… casting down imaginations…" This is a process. This is not a moment of confrontation; this is a work of transformation. Internal giants must be dismantled piece by piece through healing, truth, and renewal.

DEFEATING VS. DISMANTLING GIANTS

Before moving further, it is critical to understand the difference between defeating a giant and dismantling a giant, because misidentifying this will cause you to fight the wrong way.

Defeating is external, confrontational, and often immediate. It involves direct action, confrontation, and force. It is both physical and spiritual, visible and measurable. Defeating deals with what is standing in front of you.

First Samuel 17:48–50 shows David confronting Goliath directly. He did not negotiate, process, or delay. He ran toward the giant and struck it down. That is defeat. Luke 10:19 says, "I give unto you power… over all the power of the enemy…" There are moments where authority must be exercised immediately and decisively.

Dismantling is internal, progressive, and transformational. It involves renewing your mind, healing your heart, and exposing hidden patterns. It is mental, spiritual, and internal. Dismantling deals with what is operating within you.

Romans 12:2 says, "Be transformed by the renewing of your mind…" Second Corinthians 10:4–5 says, "…pulling down strongholds… casting down imaginations…" This is not a one-time moment. This is a process. Ephesians 4:22–24 speaks of putting off the old man and being renewed in the spirit of your mind. That is dismantling.

The key difference is this: defeat happens from the outside, while dismantling happens from the inside out. Some giants fall in a moment, while others are broken over time. Some require confrontation, while others require transformation.

If you try to defeat what must be dismantled, you will become frustrated. If you try to dismantle what must be defeated, you will delay victory.

STRONGHOLD / GENERATIONAL GIANTS MUST BE DISPLACED

Displacement is not the same as defeat. You can defeat something and still be living in its residue. You can confront it and still be influenced by it. Displacement means it no longer has permission, position, or influence.

Deuteronomy 3:2 says, "…I have delivered him into thy hand…" God gave Israel victory over Og, but they still had to take the land connected to him. Deuteronomy 7:22 says, "The Lord thy God will put out those nations before thee by little and little…"

Generational things are rarely removed instantly. They are removed progressively through obedience. Judges 1:28 says, "They did not utterly drive them out…" This is where many people miss it. They fought, they won battles, but they did not fully remove what remained. Joshua 15:63 says, "…they could not drive them out…" And because they didn't displace them, they had to coexist with what was supposed to be removed.

What displacement requires is total removal, not partial victory. You cannot negotiate with a generational pattern. Second Corinthians 10:4–5 says, "…pulling down strongholds…" It also requires replacing what was there. Matthew 12:43–45 shows that an empty place invites return. If you remove dysfunction but don't establish truth, it comes back stronger. It requires consistent enforcement. Galatians 5:1 says, "Stand fast… be not entangled again…" Displacement is maintained, not just initiated.

The reality is generational giants don't just fight you; they try to live through you. So, displacement is about breaking the pattern and removing the permission.

SEASONAL / STRATEGIC GIANTS MUST BE NAVIGATED

Now this is where maturity shows up. Some giants are not there to live with you, they are there to test, stretch, or transition you.

Second Samuel 21:15 says, "And David waxed faint…" The attack didn't come because David was weak in identity. It came because he was weary in a season. Ecclesiastes 3:1 says, "To everything there is a season…" Which means not every battle is permanent.

Some are season-specific. First Chronicles 14:14–15 says, "Thou shalt not go up after them… fetch a compass behind them…" Same enemy, different strategy. Exodus 13:17 shows that God did not lead them the short way "lest peradventure the people repent when they see war…" Timing matters.

What navigation requires is discernment of timing. Hebrews 5:14 says, "…discern both good and evil…" You have to know if this is something to fight now or move around. It requires sensitivity to strategy. Isaiah 30:21 says, "This is the way, walk ye in it…"

Not every giant is attacked head-on. It requires strength awareness. Isaiah 40:31 says, "They that wait… shall renew their strength…" Some battles are lost not because of the giant, but because of exhaustion. It requires obedience over assumption. Joshua 6 versus Joshua 8 shows Jericho required a shout and the walls fell, while Ai required strategy, positioning, and ambush. Same people, different instructions.

FINAL REVELATION

Now your framework becomes complete. Identity giants must be defeated, where truth replaces lies. Internal giants must be dismantled, where healing breaks cycles. Stronghold / generational giants must be displaced, where they are removed and replaced. Seasonal / strategic giants must be navigated, where they are discerned and handled by timing and strategy.

WHAT THIS PROTECTS YOU FROM

This protects you from treating a seasonal battle like a permanent problem, treating a generational stronghold like a one-time fight, using the wrong strategy for the wrong giant, and repeating cycles because you never fully displaced them.

THE BIG IDEA

Every giant is not just about strength. It is about strategy. Because victory is not just can you fight, it is do you know how this fight must be handled.

A CRITICAL REMINDER

A giant is not a sign that you should run. A giant is not an indication that you are out of place. A giant is not proof that you missed God

A giant is an announcement. It is an announcement that you are in the right place, you are in the promise, and you have crossed over. Because when the children of Israel entered the Promised Land, the giants were already there.

Revelation: Giants don't show up to stop you, they show up because something valuable is in front of you.

WHY GIANTS EXIST

Giants exist because there is territory worth possessing, there is promise worth fighting for, and there is purpose on the other side. And in many cases, the enemy anticipates your success. He sees your potential, your calling, and your capacity—and he positions resistance accordingly. The size of the giant often reveals the value of the promise.

FINAL CHARGE

You are not entering this volume as a victim; you are entering as a warrior.

You are not preparing to run. You are preparing to possess. Every giant you are about to encounter has a strategy attached to it. And now, you will identify them, you will confront them, and you will dismantle or destroy them. Because what God promised, you will possess.

INTRODUCTION

There is a reason this volume is called Giants in the Land.

Giants do not appear randomly. They appear where there is promise. They appear where there is purpose. They appear where there is inheritance. Throughout Scripture, every time God's people moved toward expansion, influence, territory, blessing, or promise, giants appeared. This is important because people mistakenly believe that resistance is evidence, they are in the wrong place. Scripture teaches the opposite. Often, resistance is confirmation that you are standing at the edge of something valuable.

The enemy does not waste resources guarding empty territory. He guards what matters. He guards purpose. He guards inheritance. He guards identity. He guards influence. He guards authority. He guards destiny. The fact that there is resistance around your calling is often proof that what you carry is valuable.

Before we can fully understand the giants in the land, however, we must first understand where giants come from. Because giants are not always fought. Many times, they are formed.

This takes us back to one of the most mysterious and powerful passages in all of Scripture.

Genesis 6:4 says, "There were giants in the earth in those days…"

Long before we meet Goliath, Og, the Anakim, or the giant clans that occupied the Promised Land, Scripture introduces us to the Nephilim. This is significant because God is showing us the root before He shows us the fruit. He is revealing the origin before He reveals the battle. He is teaching us how giants are made.

The Nephilim were the product of mixture. They were the result of what happens when God's design becomes corrupted. Throughout Scripture, mixture consistently produces distortion. It is the mixture of spirit and flesh. The mixture of purity and compromise. The mixture of obedience and self-will. The mixture of calling and carnality. The mixture of God's instructions and man's opinions.

This matters because many of the giants we fight today are still being formed through mixture.

Whenever something spiritual is handled carnally, mixture occurs. Whenever purpose loses consecration, mixture occurs. Whenever identity becomes distorted, mixture occurs. Whenever gifts operate without character, mixture occurs. Whenever platform grows faster than process, mixture occurs. Whenever influence exceeds maturity, mixture occurs. Whenever success grows without accountability, mixture occurs.

And mixture always creates something bigger than it was supposed to be.

That is the danger of giants. Giants are often overgrown things. Overgrown fears. Overgrown insecurities. Overgrown appetites. Overgrown trauma. Overgrown pride. Overgrown ambition. Overgrown systems. Overgrown flesh. Something that was never properly governed eventually grows beyond healthy boundaries and begins demanding more territory than it was ever designed to occupy.

One of the clearest examples of God's process for preventing mixture is found in Habakkuk 2:2. The Lord said, "Write the vision, and make it plain upon tables, that he may run that readeth it."

This verse is often quoted when people talk about vision, goals, and planning, but there is far more happening in the text than simply writing something down. The word "write" carries the idea of engraving, recording, inscribing, and legally establishing something. In other words, God was not merely telling Habakkuk to take notes. He was telling him to legally ordain, establish, and document what God had revealed.

Vision always begins with something God says before it becomes something we see. True vision is not simply human ambition. True vision originates with God. Vision is the ability to perceive what God is revealing before it becomes visible in the natural realm. It is heaven's picture of a future reality.

Scripture tells us in 1 Corinthians 2:9, "Eye hath not seen, nor ear heard, neither have entered into the heart of man, the things which God hath prepared for them that love him." Yet the following verses reveal that God reveals those things by His Spirit. Before God manifests something through us, He often reveals it to us.

One of the primary vehicles God uses to reveal His thoughts is the imagination. Unfortunately, many believers have been taught to view imagination negatively because of a misunderstanding of Scripture. We often quote, "Casting down imaginations…" without finishing the verse. Second Corinthians 10:5 is not condemning all imagination. It specifically speaks of imaginations and arguments that exalt themselves against the knowledge of God. The issue is not imagination itself. The issue is imagination operating contrary to God's truth.

Imagination is a gift from God. In many ways, imagination is the workshop of vision. It is where God's thoughts begin taking shape within us. The word itself points to the formation of an image. Before a building is constructed, someone imagines it. Before a book is written, someone sees it. Before a song is recorded, someone hears it. Before a ministry expands, someone perceives it. Before a solution is manifested, someone first receives the image.

God often places a picture in your spirit before He places it in your hands.

This is especially important for creatives because creativity begins with the ability to perceive what does not yet exist. Every painting, business, ministry, invention, book, song, strategy, and solution first existed as an image before it existed as a manifestation.

God gives vision through revelation. Revelation creates imagination. Imagination forms perception. Perception influences movement. Movement produces manifestation.

That is why Habakkuk was told not only to write the vision but also to make it plain.

Most people interpret "plain" as simply making it easy to read. While clarity is certainly part of the meaning, the concept goes deeper. The vision had to remain pure. It had to remain unmixed. It had to remain uncontaminated by fear, pride, insecurity, self-will, comparison, carnality, or compromise.

And this brings us right back to the central issue of giants.

Mixture creates giants.

When God gives a word and we add flesh to it, mixture occurs. When God gives vision but we substitute our own agenda, mixture occurs. When God gives instruction but we ignore strategy, mixture occurs.

When God gives revelation but we reject consecration, mixture occurs. When we hear the word but fail to seek God's process, mixture occurs.

Many people receive a promise but never pursue the strategy attached to the promise. They hear a word but never obtain understanding. They receive vision but never develop discipline. They receive revelation but never pursue maturity.

God's vision is pure.

The challenge is keeping it pure as it moves through us.

Whenever vision becomes mixed with flesh, a giant is formed. Whenever purpose becomes mixed with pride, a giant is formed. Whenever gifting becomes mixed with ego, a giant is formed. Whenever influence becomes mixed with insecurity, a giant is formed.

This is why consecration matters.

Before Israel entered the Promised Land, God required circumcision at Gilgal because flesh had to be cut away before promise could be possessed. They could not enter covenant territory carrying uncircumcised flesh and expect to properly steward what God was giving them. The cutting represented separation, purification, consecration, and covenant alignment.

The principle remains true today. Flesh unmanaged always creates giants. Many of the battles creatives face today have been formed through mixture. Gift without discipline. Platform without healing. Creativity without clarity. Influence without instruction. Performance without intimacy. Movement without identity. Visibility without accountability. Ambition without submission.

What was meant to equip has often become entertainment. What was meant to minister has often become performance. What was meant to build people has often become branding. What was meant to glorify God has often become self-promotion. As a result, many creatives find themselves exhausted, frustrated, overwhelmed, and spiritually depleted because they are operating from mixture instead of consecration.

This volume shifts our focus to the actual giants named in Scripture. These are the giants that occupied territories, opposed God's people, and stood between promise and possession. We will explore the giant clans, the cities they occupied, the kings they served, the systems they built, and the spiritual patterns they represent.

Together we will examine who these giants were, what their names mean, where they lived, what they represented, how they operated, how they still manifest today, and most importantly, how to crush them.

Because these giants are not merely ancient enemies from biblical history. They are patterns. They are systems. They are strongholds. They are spiritual realities that continue to influence people today. And if we do not understand the pattern, we will continue repeating the battle.

One of the most important revelations you must carry throughout this volume is this:

Giants are not proof that you are in the wrong place. They are proof that you are in the land. The presence of giants is confirmation of promise. The presence of warfare is often confirmation of value. The presence of resistance is often confirmation of assignment.

Many people spend so much time focusing on the giant that they forget what the giant is standing in front of. Giants never appear in front of worthless territory. They stand in front of promise. They stand in front of inheritance. They stand in front of destiny. They stand in front of influence. They stand in front of purpose.

That is why this volume is not about retreat. It is about possession. It is about consecration. It is about clarity. It is about authority. It is about learning how to war correctly. Because not every giant is conquered the same way. Some giants must be defeated. Some must be dismantled. Some must be displaced. Some must be driven out gradually. Some must be completely destroyed. But every giant can be overcome. And every giant that stands between you and God's promise can be crushed.

So, we begin where giants began. We begin at the root. We begin with the Nephilim.

THE NEPHILIM

The Giant of Mixture / Corruption

Scriptures: Genesis 6:1–4, Numbers 13:33

Meaning: "Fallen Ones", "Those Who Cause Others to Fall", Giants

CONTEXT

Before we can fully understand the giants in the land, we must first understand where giants come from. Because giants are not just fought. Many times, they are formed.

The first direct mention of giants in Scripture is not Goliath. It is not the Anakim. It is not Og or the Philistines. The first mention of giants appears in Genesis 6 with the Nephilim. Before giants became external battles, they first became internal corruption. The Nephilim reveal the origin of mixture, distortion, compromise, and abnormal development.

Genesis 6:4 says, "There were giants in the earth in those days…" The word Nephilim is commonly connected to the meanings "fallen ones," "those who cause others to fall," or simply "giants." This is significant because anything that falls from original design eventually becomes distorted. God never intended corruption. God never intended mixture. God never intended flesh to overpower spirit. Yet mixture created giants.

The Nephilim represent what happens when things that were meant to remain consecrated become corrupted through mixture. They represent compromise, distortion, misalignment, and flesh ruling over spirit. This is the giant created when gifts outgrow character, when platform grows faster than process, when influence increases without maturity, and when talent develops without consecration.

ROOT OF THIS GIANT

This giant is rooted in compromise, corruption, distortion, mixture, lack of consecration, flesh overpowering spirit, partial obedience, pride, and lack of accountability.

Mixture always produces something bigger than it was meant to be.

That is the danger of giants. Giants are often overgrown things. Overgrown appetites. Overgrown flesh. Overgrown pride. Overgrown insecurity. Overgrown ambition. Overgrown trauma. Overgrown systems. Something that was never properly governed eventually grows beyond healthy boundaries.

This giant is dangerous because mixture often looks powerful at first. It can look productive. It can look successful. It can look gifted. But underneath the surface, instability is growing. This is why some people can be extremely gifted and still deeply broken. Some can have visibility but no stability. Some can have charisma without character. Some can have influence without discipline.

Gifting and consecration are not the same thing.

WHAT THIS GIANT DOES

The Nephilim giant distorts identity, purpose, priorities, boundaries, discipline, and spiritual clarity.

This giant thrives in environments where boundaries disappear, discipline weakens, accountability fades, truth becomes compromised, and flesh is left unchecked.

The Nephilim giant operates through compromise, pride, impatience, partial obedience, lack of accountability, and flesh driven decisions.

Partial obedience is still disobedience.

FOR CREATIVES

This is one of the greatest dangers facing creatives today. Creatives often carry deep sensitivity, influence, emotional depth, prophetic insight, visibility, and gifting. But if those things are not properly stewarded, mixture develops.

This looks like gifting without healing, branding without character, influence without accountability, creativity without discipline, performance without intimacy, assignment becoming ego, and platform replacing presence. What begins in the spirit can become corrupted in the flesh if it is not consecrated.

Many creatives are exhausted because they are operating from mixture instead of alignment. What was meant to equip has become entertainment. What was meant to minister has become performance. What was meant to build people has become branding.

The danger is not simply that people lose focus. The danger is that mixture slowly becomes normalized.

SIGNS YOU MAY BE DEALING WITH THE NEPHILIM GIANT

One of the most dangerous things about the Nephilim giant is that many people do not recognize it because mixture often looks powerful before it becomes destructive. Mixture can look productive. It can look gifted. It can look successful. It can even look spiritual on the surface while corruption is quietly growing underneath.

This giant is subtle because it does not always start with obvious rebellion. Many times, it starts with small compromises, partial obedience, blurred boundaries, distorted priorities, flesh driven decisions, and slowly moving away from God's original design. Over time, mixture grows until it begins producing instability, confusion, exhaustion, and distortion.

So how do you know you may be dealing with the Nephilim giant?

One of the first signs is confusion of identity. When this giant is operating, people often lose clarity concerning who they are, what they are assigned to, and what God actually said. They begin comparing themselves constantly, shifting directions frequently, chasing platforms instead of purpose, and struggling to stay grounded in their identity. Mixture distorts self-perception.

Another sign is when gifting becomes stronger than character. You may still be productive, talented, visible, and effective outwardly, but internally there is inconsistency, instability, emotional imbalance, pride, hidden compromise, or lack of discipline. This giant thrives when people develop gifts but neglect healing, maturity, accountability, and consecration.

A major sign of this giant is performance replacing presence. You begin focusing more on appearance than intimacy with God. Ministry becomes performance. Worship becomes production. Creativity becomes branding. Assignment becomes ego. Instead of creating from overflow, you begin creating from pressure, comparison, or the need for validation.

Another sign is constant compromise of boundaries. When the Nephilim giant is operating, boundaries weaken. People start justifying things they once had conviction about. Discipline decreases. Prayer becomes inconsistent. Time in the Word becomes shallow. Flesh begins leading decisions instead of the Spirit.

This giant also creates abnormal appetites. You may notice excessive ambition, unhealthy craving for attention, addiction to affirmation, obsession with visibility, inability to rest, emotional instability, and constant striving.

Mixture always creates imbalance.

For creatives specifically, this giant often appears as burnout, creating without peace, producing while emotionally empty, constantly feeling pressured to perform, losing the joy of creating, and feeling disconnected from God while remaining active publicly.

You can be functioning publicly while slowly deteriorating privately.

Another major sign is hidden inconsistency. What people see publicly and who you are privately become two different people. This giant feeds on hidden things because mixture grows where there is no accountability.

You may also notice chronic instability. Constant emotional highs and lows. Constant starting and stopping. Constant inconsistency. Constant drifting. The Nephilim giant produces things that become oversized but unstable at the same time.

This giant also creates spiritual dullness. Conviction weakens. Discernment decreases. Sensitivity to God fades. People begin operating off talent, habit, charisma, and gifting instead of intimacy with God.

And one of the clearest signs is exhaustion without fruitfulness. You are doing more, carrying more, producing more, striving more, but there is no real peace, fulfillment, stability, or sustainability attached to it. Because mixture always demands more flesh. That is why this giant must be confronted quickly. Left unchecked, mixture eventually grows into corruption, instability, and destruction.

But the good news is this:

The fact that you recognize the signs means you are already confronting the giant. And what is exposed can be healed. What is identified can be corrected. And what mixture created, consecration can crush.

HOW TO CRUSH THIS GIANT

The first step to crushing the giant of mixture is returning to consecration. Consecration means separation unto God. It means setting yourself apart again. Before there is platform, there must be process. Before there is influence, there must be integrity. Before there is promise, there must be purification.

1 Samuel 16:5 - "Sanctify yourselves..."

Consecration was preparation for encounter. Consecration protects calling. Many people want visibility without purification, but visibility without consecration becomes dangerous. God is not simply looking for gifted people. He is looking for governed people.

Consecration is practical. It means reevaluating what has access to your life. It means examining your habits, your environments, your conversations, your relationships, your entertainment, your motives, and your patterns.

It means asking difficult questions:

What is feeding my spirit? What is feeding my flesh? What is pulling me closer to God? What is pulling me away from Him? You cannot consistently feed flesh and expect spirit to stay strong.

Galatians 5:16

"Walk in the Spirit, and ye shall not fulfil the lust of the flesh."

The flesh must be governed. Undisciplined flesh eventually creates giants. This is why spiritual disciplines such as prayer, fasting, worship, rest, accountability, and time in the Word matter. These things are not religious rituals. They are systems of spiritual strength.

One of the greatest ways to crush mixture is restoring clarity. Mixture creates confusion. Clarity restores alignment. You must know who you are, what God said, what belongs to you, and what does not belong to you.

Many people are fighting battles simply because they have lost clarity concerning identity and assignment.

This is why the enemy attack's identity so aggressively. If he can distort identity, he can distort movement. If he can distort movement, he can delay purpose.

Numbers 13:33 - "We were in our own sight as grasshoppers…"

Before Israel lost territory externally, they first lost identity internally. You cannot defeat giants while thinking small about yourself. You must renew your mind with truth. You must remind yourself that you are chosen, called, fearfully and wonderfully made, the head and not the tail, above only and not beneath. Identity matters because perception shapes movement.

Another way to crush this giant is rebuilding boundaries. Boundaries prevent contamination. Not everything deserves access to your spirit, your emotions, your creativity, your mind, or your body.

Proverbs 4:23 - "Keep thy heart with all diligence; for out of it are the issues of life."

To "keep" means to guard. Boundaries are not punishment. Boundaries are protection. For creatives especially, boundaries are critical because creatives often absorb environments deeply. What you constantly expose yourself to eventually shapes your thinking, your creativity, and your appetite. If you do not guard your environment, your environment will eventually govern you.

Crushing this giant also requires accountability. Isolation strengthens mixture. Hidden things grow in darkness. This is why confession, community, mentorship, counseling, and healthy leadership matter.

James 5:16 - "Confess your faults one to another, and pray one for another, that ye may be healed."

Healing grows where honesty exists. Another practical strategy is slowing down long enough to allow process to mature you. Many people want immediate visibility, but immature success creates unstable foundations. Sometimes God slows things down because He is protecting you from becoming successful before you are spiritually prepared to sustain it. Process protects purpose.

Finally, you must return to God's original design. The goal is not simply influence. The goal is alignment. The goal is not just gifting. The goal is maturity. The goal is not visibility. The goal is obedience.

Romans 12:2

"Be not conformed to this world: but be ye transformed by the renewing of your mind..."

Transformation happens when your mind is renewed and your spirit realigns with truth. The more your mind aligns with God's design, the weaker mixture becomes.

Many of the giants people are fighting today were formed through years of mixture. Years of compromise. Years of ignoring boundaries. Years of operating in gifting without healing. Years of platform without process.

But what mixture created, consecration can crush. You are not powerless against this giant. Through discipline, consecration, accountability, clarity, healing, and obedience, this giant can be dismantled. The same God who calls you also equips you to walk in purity, alignment, and truth.

PROPHETIC INSIGHT

The Nephilim reveal where giants begin. But they also reveal something powerful: If giants can be formed... they can also be destroyed.

PRAYERS FOR CRUSHING THE NEPHILIM GIANT

Prayer of Consecration

Father, in the name of Jesus, I come before You asking You to search me, cleanse me, purify me, and realign me with Your original design for my life. Expose every area of compromise, mixture, distortion, pride, rebellion, partial obedience, and flesh driven thinking operating within me. Remove everything that has contaminated my spirit, weakened my discernment, and distorted my identity.

Lord, I renounce every place where gifting became more important than character, where platform became more important than process, and where performance replaced intimacy with You. Forgive me for every area where I operated in my own strength, my own ambition, my own timing, or my own desires instead of fully surrendering to Your will.

Create in me a clean heart and renew a right spirit within me. Restore clarity to my mind, purity to my motives, discipline to my life, and integrity to my character. Teach me to walk in consecration, obedience, humility, and truth.

Father, cut away every area of flesh that has grown beyond healthy boundaries. Circumcise my heart. Purify my thoughts. Govern my appetites. Strengthen my discipline. Restore my sensitivity to Your voice.

I declare that I will not be governed by flesh, culture, pressure, ego, or compromise. I will be led by Your Spirit. Let every giant formed through mixture, compromise, distortion, trauma, insecurity, pride, or lack of accountability be dismantled in the name of Jesus.

I choose purity over popularity.

I choose obedience over applause.

I choose consecration over compromise.

I choose Your presence over performance.

In Jesus' name, amen.

Prayer for Creatives

Father, I surrender my gifts, creativity, influence, platform, voice, and assignment back to You. Help me create from intimacy and not insecurity. Deliver me from striving, comparison, competition, performance, validation seeking, and emotional exhaustion.

Teach me to steward what You placed inside of me with wisdom, discipline, maturity, and integrity. Protect my creativity from corruption. Protect my assignment from ego. Protect my heart from pride. Protect my mind from confusion.

Heal every area where mixture entered through wounds, rejection, trauma, pressure, or lack of boundaries. Restore joy to my creativity. Restore peace to my process. Restore purity to my motives.

I declare that my gifts will glorify God and not my flesh. My creativity will be governed by truth. My influence will be covered by integrity. My platform will remain surrendered to God.

In Jesus' name, amen.

Prayer for Purity & Clarity

Father, remove every confusing voice from my life. Silence every influence that is pulling me away from Your truth. Help me discern what belongs to me and what does not. Restore clarity concerning my identity, assignment, purpose, and direction.

Renew my mind according to Romans 12:2. Let every distorted thought pattern be broken. Let every false identity fall. Let every mindset formed through fear, rejection, insecurity, trauma, comparison, or compromise be uprooted.

I declare that my mind belongs to God. My spirit belongs to God. My body belongs to God. My gifts belong to God.

I will walk in alignment.

I will walk in purity.

I will walk in wisdom.

I will walk in truth.

In Jesus' name, amen.

DECLARATIONS FOR CRUSHING THE NEPHILIM GIANT

- I renounce every form of mixture, compromise, and distortion operating in my life.
- I will not allow flesh to rule over spirit.
- I am consecrated, set apart, and aligned with God's purpose for my life.
- I will not trade purity for popularity.
- I will not trade intimacy for influence.
- I will not trade process for platform.
- I am governed by the Spirit of God.
- My gifts will not outgrow my character.
- My platform will not exceed my maturity.
- My influence will remain covered by integrity.
- I break agreement with compromise, confusion, instability, pride, and flesh driven decisions.
- I declare that hidden things are being exposed and healed.
- I declare that my mind is being renewed.
- I declare that my identity is secure in Christ.
- I am chosen.

I am called.
I am fearfully and wonderfully made.
I am the head and not the tail.
I am above only and not beneath.

- I will not create from insecurity, pressure, comparison, or ego.
- I will create from overflow, intimacy, healing, and truth.
- My creativity will glorify God.
- My purpose will not be corrupted by mixture.
- My assignment will not be destroyed by compromise.
- I have clarity.

I have discipline.
I have wisdom.
I have discernment.
I have healthy boundaries.

- What mixture created, consecration will crush.
- Every giant formed through compromise, distortion, corruption, insecurity, trauma, pride, and flesh must fall.
- I will walk in purity.

I will walk in alignment.
I will walk in obedience.
I will walk in truth. And every giant in my life will be crushed.

SISERA

The Giant of Oppression, Trauma, & Intimidation

Scriptures: Judges 4–5

Meaning: Sisera is commonly connected to meanings involving:

battle array, seeing horse, military oppression, organized intimidation
Sisera was not just a man. He represented an oppressive system.

This giant represents: oppression, fear, control, trauma, intimidation, psychological warfare

emotional exhaustion, silencing, survival mode

CONTEXT

After understanding the Nephilim and how giants are formed through mixture, compromise, distortion, and corruption, we now encounter another type of giant warfare in Scripture: the Sisera giant. While the Nephilim reveal where giants begin, Sisera reveals what happens when oppression is allowed to continue unchecked for too long.

The Sisera giant is one of the most oppressive giants in Scripture because it operates through intimidation, fear, control, trauma, and prolonged oppression. Sisera was the commander of Jabin's army, and for twenty years Israel lived under harsh oppression and psychological warfare.

This giant is dangerous because it does not always attack suddenly. Many times, it attacks gradually.

It wears people down over time. It creates exhaustion, fear, silence, intimidation, and emotional paralysis until people begin adapting to oppression instead of confronting it. The Sisera giant thrives when people become accustomed to surviving instead of living free.

One of the most dangerous things about this giant is that it conditions people to normalize dysfunction. People begin functioning while wounded, smiling while exhausted, leading while traumatized, and surviving while inwardly broken. Over time, oppression leaves residue.

Sisera operated through intimidation and fear. He wanted Israel psychologically defeated before they were ever defeated physically. This is why this giant attacks the mind so heavily. One of the biggest signs you may be dealing with the Sisera giant is constant intimidation. You feel pressure, fear, anxiety, or emotional heaviness before conversations, opportunities, decisions, assignments, or transitions. You constantly feel mentally "pressed." This giant attempts to make you feel powerless, voiceless, small, unsupported, or incapable.

Another major sign is emotional exhaustion from prolonged warfare. Sisera oppressed Israel for twenty years. Long term pressure changes people when healing does not take place properly. This giant often leaves people mentally tired, emotionally drained, hyper alert, guarded, defensive, and constantly expecting conflict.

This giant creates trauma responses.

You may notice shutting down emotionally, fear of confrontation, avoiding conflict at all costs, difficulty trusting people, living in survival mode, always preparing for the worst, overreacting because of previous wounds, and difficulty resting or relaxing. The Sisera giant often leaves people functioning externally while inwardly exhausted.

The Sisera giant also creates cycles of fear and control. This can show up in unhealthy leadership, toxic church environments, manipulative relationships, controlling systems, abusive authority, or environments where people feel silenced, intimidated, emotionally trapped, or constantly fearful of making mistakes.

WHAT THIS GIANT DOES

The Sisera giant attacks the mind, emotions, confidence, movement, and sense of safety.

This giant:

wears people down emotionally, creates fear-based decisions, produces hyper vigilance, causes emotional paralysis, normalizes survival mode, silences voices, creates intimidation, conditions people to settle

This giant wants people functioning externally while internally exhausted. It wants people surviving instead of possessing promise.

Another major sign of the Sisera giant is chronic overthinking and mental torment. Sisera operated through military intimidation. He wanted Israel psychologically exhausted before battle ever began. This giant floods the mind with fear scenarios, "what if" thinking, dread, insecurity, intimidation, and constant expectation of negative outcomes.

This giant also creates learned helplessness. After prolonged oppression, people begin believing freedom is impossible. They stop fighting. They stop dreaming. They stop expecting change. They stop believing breakthrough is possible. They begin surviving instead of possessing promise. That is one of the most dangerous effects of this giant. It conditions people to settle.

Another major sign is feeling emotionally stuck after trauma. The Sisera giant often leaves unresolved pain buried beneath the surface. People continue functioning outwardly while inwardly carrying fear, grief, anger, distrust, disappointment, and emotional heaviness. Trauma may be hidden, but it still influences movement.

This giant also attacks confidence and movement. You may notice hesitation whenever God calls you forward. Every new level feels dangerous. Every transition feels threatening. Every opportunity feels risky because trauma has trained your nervous system to expect pain instead of promise.

One of the clearest signs of this giant is when your nervous system never feels safe. Even during peaceful moments, internally you still feel pressure, tension, fear, anxiety, or emotional alertness. Your body may be resting, but your mind remains in battle mode.

Because oppression leaves residue.

FOR CREATIVES

For creatives, this giant is especially dangerous because creatives are often highly sensitive emotionally and spiritually. This giant attacks creatives through fear of expression, fear of being misunderstood, fear of rejection, feeling silenced, feeling unsupported, creating from pressure instead of freedom, shrinking creatively to avoid conflict, and hiding gifts because of previous wounds.

This giant convinces people that staying quiet is safer than being authentic.

Many creatives stop creating freely because trauma has trained them to associate visibility with pain. They become cautious, guarded, hesitant, and afraid to fully express what God placed inside of them. The enemy understands that if he can silence your voice, he can delay your assignment.

Creatives dealing with this giant often: overthink everything they release, fear criticism, hide their true voice,

delay opportunities, shrink in rooms they were called to lead, create from anxiety instead of overflow, disconnect emotionally from their gifts

This giant wants creatives intimidated instead of impactful. It wants their voice silenced before their assignment reaches people.

SIGNS YOU MAY BE DEALING WITH THE SISERA GIANT

One of the biggest signs is constant intimidation. You feel pressure, fear, or anxiety before conversations, opportunities, decisions, transitions, or assignments. You constantly feel mentally "pressed." This giant attempts to make you feel small, powerless, voiceless, or incapable.

Another sign is emotional exhaustion from prolonged warfare. Sisera oppressed Israel for twenty years. Long term pressure changes people if they do not heal properly. This giant often leaves people mentally tired, emotionally drained, hyper alert, guarded, and constantly expecting conflict.

This giant creates trauma responses.

You may notice: shutting down emotionally, fear of confrontation, avoiding conflict at all costs, difficulty trusting people, living in survival mode, always preparing for the worst, overreacting because of previous wounds, difficulty resting or relaxing

The Sisera giant often creates cycles of fear and control. This can show up in unhealthy leadership, toxic environments, manipulative relationships, or systems where people feel silenced, intimidated, or emotionally trapped.

Another sign is chronic overthinking and mental torment. Sisera operated through military intimidation. He wanted Israel psychologically defeated before they ever fought physically.

This giant constantly floods the mind with fear scenarios, worst case thinking, intimidation, insecurity and dread.

This giant also creates learned helplessness. After prolonged oppression, people begin believing freedom is impossible. They stop fighting. They stop dreaming. They stop expecting change. They begin surviving instead of possessing promise.

Another major sign is feeling emotionally stuck after trauma. The Sisera giant often leaves unresolved pain buried beneath the surface. People continue functioning outwardly while inwardly carrying fear, grief, anger, distrust, and emotional heaviness.

And one of the clearest signs is when your nervous system never feels safe. Even during peace, your mind stays in battle mode. Your body may be resting, but internally you still feel pressure, fear, tension, or emotional alertness. Because oppression leaves residue.

HOW TO CRUSH THIS GIANT

The good news is this: Sisera was defeated. Not only was he defeated, his oppressive system collapsed with him. The very thing that terrorized Israel for years eventually fell. Which means intimidation can be broken, trauma can heal, fear can lose its grip, oppressive cycles can end, and peace can return.

The first step in crushing the Sisera giant is recognizing that prolonged oppression is not God's design for your life. Many people become so accustomed to surviving that they no longer pursue freedom.

John 10:10 - "I am come that they might have life, and that they might have it more abundantly."

God did not create you merely to survive trauma. He created you to heal from it.

The second step is confronting fear instead of partnering with it. Fear grows when it remains unchallenged.

2 Timothy 1:7 - "For God hath not given us the spirit of fear; but of power, and of love, and of a sound mind."

Fear is not your inheritance. Power is. Love is. A sound mind is.

A sound mind matters because trauma often fragments thinking. Trauma causes people to expect danger everywhere. But healing restores stability. Healing restores safety. Healing restores trust.

Another way to crush this giant is through truth and exposure. Oppression thrives in silence. Trauma thrives in hidden places. But healing grows where honesty exists.

James 5:16 - "Confess your faults one to another, and pray one for another, that ye may be healed."

Many people want healing privately while continuing to suffer silently. But freedom often requires safe community, accountability, counseling, mentorship, prayer, and support.

This is why therapy, counseling, and emotional healing matter. Spiritual warfare and emotional healing are not enemies. Sometimes God heals spiritually, emotionally, mentally, and naturally all at the same time. Healing is holistic.

Another practical way to crush this giant is rebuilding your voice. Trauma often silences people. Oppression convinces people their voice does not matter. But your voice carries authority. Your creativity carries authority. Your assignment carries authority.

For creatives, this means learning how to create from healing instead of pain. It means allowing God to restore joy, expression, confidence, and freedom. It means refusing to allow fear to shrink your creativity or silence your purpose.

You must also stop living in constant survival mode. Survival mode may help you endure temporarily, but it was never meant to become your permanent lifestyle.

Isaiah 26:3 - "Thou wilt keep him in perfect peace, whose mind is stayed on thee..."

Peace is not simply the absence of warfare. Peace is stability in the middle of it. Rest is also critical in crushing this giant because prolonged oppression exhausts the nervous system.

Matthew 11:28 - "Come unto me, all ye that labor and are heavy laden, and I will give you rest."

Rest restores what trauma drained.

You must also reclaim movement. Trauma often causes hesitation, delay, fear of risk, and fear of transition. But progress is part of healing. Even small steps forward matter. The enemy wants you frozen, but healing requires movement.

Deborah and Barak eventually confronted Sisera directly. This is important because some giants do not leave until they are confronted. Avoidance prolongs oppression. But courage breaks cycles.

And one of the most powerful revelations in this story is that the giant Israel feared eventually fell through unexpected strategy. God often uses unusual methods to overthrow oppressive systems. Which means your healing may not look like someone else's healing. Your recovery may not look traditional. Your process may not look familiar. But freedom is still possible.

The Sisera giant wants you intimidated, exhausted, traumatized, silent, fearful, emotionally trapped, and constantly surviving.

But God wants you healed. God wants you free. God wants you restored. God wants your voice back.

And what oppression tried to silence, God can restore.

PRAYERS FOR CRUSHING THE SISERA GIANT

Father, in the name of Jesus, I renounce every spirit of intimidation, oppression, fear, trauma, emotional exhaustion, and control operating in my life. I refuse to live in survival mode. I refuse to normalize dysfunction. Heal every wounded place in me that prolonged warfare has affected.

Lord, restore my mind, emotions, confidence, peace, and stability. Remove every residue of trauma, fear, rejection, disappointment, grief, and emotional heaviness. Heal my nervous system from constant stress and hyper vigilance.

I break agreement with fear, intimidation, silence, insecurity, and emotional paralysis. I declare that I will no longer shrink back, hide my voice, or suppress my assignment because of previous pain.

Teach me how to heal properly. Surround me with safe community, wise counsel, accountability, and support. Restore my ability to trust, rest, create, lead, and move forward again.

Father, restore my joy. Restore my confidence. Restore my peace.

Restore my voice.

What oppression tried to silence, restore in greater strength.

In Jesus' name, amen.

DECLARATIONS FOR CRUSHING THE SISERA GIANT

- I will not live intimidated.
- I will not live emotionally trapped.
- I will not remain in survival mode.
- I break agreement with fear, oppression, trauma, emotional exhaustion, and intimidation.
- I have power.

I have love.

I have a sound mind.

- I am healing emotionally, mentally, spiritually, and naturally.
- My mind is stable.

My heart is healing.
My voice is returning.
My confidence is being restored.

- I will not allow trauma to silence my assignment.
- I will not allow fear to stop my movement.
- I will create freely.

I will speak boldly.
I will move forward confidently.

- God is restoring every place oppression tried to break.
- I will not settle for survival when God promised freedom.
- I am free.

I am healing.
I am whole.
I am restored.

- And every Sisera giant operating in my life must fall.

JABIN

The Giant of Oppressive Intelligence

Scripture: Judges 4:1–24

Meaning: "He understands," "the wise one," or "one who is intelligent"

CONTEXT

Jabin was the king of Canaan who reigned in Hazor. The Bible says that he "mightily oppressed the children of Israel" for twenty years. Jabin represents the giant of oppressive intelligence. This is not merely strength; this is strategy. This is a system. This is a mind that knows how to control, manipulate, dominate, and keep people bound. Jabin did not fight alone. He had Sisera, the commander of his army, and nine hundred chariots of iron. This means he had leadership, military power, technology, intimidation, and systems working on his behalf.

This giant is dangerous because it is not always loud at first. It studies. It calculates. It builds systems of control. It understands weaknesses and uses them against people. Jabin represents the giant of oppressive wisdom, controlling systems, and strategic bondage. This is the giant that knows how to keep people stuck. It understands your patterns. It understands your fears. It understands how to use intimidation. It understands how to build systems that make freedom feel impossible. Jabin is the giant that says, "I know how to keep you under this."

Some giants do not just attack your emotions; they attack your structure. They attack your mind. They attack your movement. They attack your ability to believe freedom is possible. Jabin represents anything that has studied you long enough to oppress you strategically. It may appear as a toxic system, generational bondage, a controlling relationship, fear that has learned your triggers, poverty that has shaped your thinking, religion that has taught limitation instead of liberty, or trauma that has trained your nervous system to expect defeat. Jabin is not random oppression. Jabin is organized oppression.

The giant of Jabin uses understanding without righteousness, knowledge without compassion, authority without justice, and systems without freedom. This giant makes people feel as though oppression is normal. It creates cycles where people stop fighting because they have been under it for so long. Israel was oppressed for twenty years. Some people were born into that oppression and thought bondage was normal. That is what Jabin does. He keeps people in a condition so long that captivity becomes familiar.

UNDERSTANDING OPPRESSIVE INTELLIGENCE

One of the most dangerous things about Jabin is that he does not always appear violent at first. He appears intelligent, reasonable, strategic, organized, and calm. That is why many people do not recognize him until they have already been controlled by him.

Jabin is the giant of oppressive intelligence. This means he uses wisdom, strategy, knowledge, systems, manipulation, intimidation, and psychological control to dominate people. This giant does not always need to scream. Sometimes he controls with silence. Sometimes he controls with pressure. Sometimes he controls through fear, guilt, confusion, intimidation, dependency, or emotional exhaustion.

Jabin studies people. He learns what moves them. He learns their weaknesses, insecurities, fears, wounds, desires, and vulnerabilities, then uses those things to maintain control. That is oppressive intelligence. It is intelligence used without righteousness, wisdom without love, knowledge without integrity, and strategy without compassion.

Oppressive intelligence knows how to make you doubt yourself. It knows how to keep you emotionally unstable. It knows how to keep you second-guessing your decisions. It knows how to keep you dependent. It knows how to make you feel trapped even when the door is open. It studies your reactions, your emotions, and your pain, then weaponizes that information against you. This giant often creates environments where people feel mentally exhausted, emotionally drained, spiritually silenced, and psychologically overwhelmed.

WHAT MIND CONTROL LOOKS LIKE

Mind control does not always look dramatic. Sometimes mind control is simply repeated manipulation over time. It occurs when someone slowly conditions you to stop trusting your own thoughts, discernment, judgment, instincts, and voice. This giant wants people mentally imprisoned before they are physically imprisoned.

It sounds like, "You're overreacting." "That never happened." "You're too emotional." "You'll never make it without me." "No one else would deal with you." "You're crazy." "You're the problem." "You always misunderstand." Over time, the person begins questioning themselves instead of questioning the oppression. That is how Jabin controls the mind.

WHAT MANIPULATION LOOKS LIKE

Manipulation is control disguised as concern. It is when someone uses emotions, guilt, fear, pressure, silence, shame, confusion, intimidation, or even kindness to control outcomes. Manipulation often appears through being overly nice when they want something, withdrawing affection when they do not get their way, using guilt to force compliance, twisting conversations, rewriting history, making you feel responsible for their behavior, playing the victim when confronted, punishing honesty, creating confusion during conflict, keeping people emotionally off balance, and giving just enough approval to keep people attached.

Manipulators know how to keep people hoping things will change while continuing the same destructive cycles. They maintain power by keeping others emotionally invested in promises that never materialize.

WHAT DOMINANCE LOOKS LIKE

Dominance is excessive control. It is the need to overpower, silence, intimidate, or govern others. A dominant Jabin spirit hates losing control. It often appears through controlling conversations, constantly interrupting people, needing the final word, using anger or intimidation to silence disagreement, making others afraid to speak honestly, micromanaging everything, controlling finances, access, opportunities, or relationships, making people feel small, using intelligence or status to overpower people, using spiritual authority incorrectly, demanding submission without accountability, and punishing independence.

A dominant spirit wants people dependent, weak, fearful, and submissive to its control. It is not interested in developing people. It is interested in managing them.

SIGNS YOU ARE DEALING WITH JABIN

One of the clearest signs that you are dealing with Jabin is that you constantly second-guess yourself. You feel emotionally exhausted around certain people. You feel mentally foggy or confused after conversations. You are afraid to speak honestly. You feel as though you are always walking on eggshells. You feel controlled but cannot fully explain why. You have lost confidence in your own discernment. You find yourself apologizing constantly. You feel trapped emotionally, mentally, spiritually, or financially. You feel drained instead of empowered. You feel fear when trying to establish boundaries. You silence yourself to avoid conflict. You feel pressure to please people in order to keep peace.

Spiritually, Jabin wants to keep people oppressed long enough that they stop fighting for freedom. This spirit attacks courage, identity, confidence, discernment, voice, and movement. It wants people spiritually paralyzed. People under this giant often know they are called but feel stuck. They hear God but fear obedience. They want freedom but feel powerless. They stay in unhealthy systems because fear has become stronger than faith. They remain silent because intimidation has trained them not to speak.

FOR CREATIVES

For creatives, Jabin often appears as systems, voices, and environments that suppress originality, innovation, imagination, and expression. A creative under Jabin may constantly second-guess every idea. They may spend more time seeking permission than creating. They may feel paralyzed by criticism. They may silence their own voice to keep others comfortable. They may become dependent upon validation before releasing what God has given them.

Jabin tells creatives that they are not ready, not qualified, not talented enough, or not good enough. This giant wants creativity imprisoned before it is ever expressed. It wants gifts buried, books unwritten, songs unsung, businesses unlaunched, ideas undeveloped, and dreams delayed. Jabin understands that if your voice is released, freedom may follow.

FOR LEADERS

For leaders, Jabin often appears as control, intimidation, fear-based leadership, micromanagement, manipulation, and unhealthy systems. Leaders under the influence of Jabin often struggle to delegate because control feels safer than trust. They may create environments where people are afraid to fail. They may use position instead of influence. They may value compliance over development. They may unintentionally reproduce the very oppression they once experienced.

Jabin loves unhealthy leadership structures because systems can often oppress more effectively than individuals. This giant creates cultures where innovation dies, voices are silenced, growth is restricted, and people remain dependent rather than developed. The goal of Kingdom leadership is empowerment. The goal of Jabin leadership is control.

THE DANGER OF JABIN

The danger of Jabin is that people can normalize oppression. After twenty years of bondage, Israel became accustomed to being controlled. That is what happens when this giant goes unchecked. People begin surviving instead of living, existing instead of thriving, managing oppression instead of confronting it, and adapting to bondage instead of pursuing freedom.

Jabin is not just a person. It is a spirit of oppressive control. It can operate through systems, families, relationships, leadership, religion, culture, workplaces, organizations, and even through internal fear patterns created by trauma.

The good news is that God always raises up a Deborah. God always sends wisdom greater than oppression. Every system of control eventually collapses when truth, courage, discernment, and obedience arise.

HOW TO CRUSH THE GIANT OF JABIN

You crush Jabin by crying out to God. Judges 4:3 says that the children of Israel cried unto the Lord. Their deliverance began when their cry went up. Some systems do not break until the oppressed open their mouths. You cannot quietly tolerate what God is trying to deliver you from.

You crush Jabin by receiving prophetic instruction. God raised up Deborah, a prophetess and judge, to provide divine strategy. Jabin had natural strategy, but Deborah carried Kingdom strategy. Oppressive wisdom must always be confronted by divine wisdom.

You crush Jabin by obeying God's direction. Deborah told Barak exactly what to do. Deliverance required movement. It was not enough to know what God said. Someone had to obey.

You crush Jabin by confronting the system behind the oppression. Sisera was Jabin's military power, but Jabin was the throne behind the torment. Many people spend their lives fighting symptoms while ignoring the system producing them. To crush Jabin, you must identify what has been empowering the bondage.

You crush Jabin by refusing intimidation. Nine hundred chariots of iron looked impossible to defeat, but what appears impossible to man is still subject to God. The weapons of the enemy do not cancel the Word of the Lord.

You crush Jabin by partnering with the right people. Deborah, Barak, and Jael all played a role in the victory. This giant was not crushed by one person alone. God used prophetic leadership, obedient action, and unexpected intervention. Some victories require divine collaboration.

SCRIPTURES

Judges 4:3 — "And the children of Israel cried unto the Lord…" Cry out. Stop suffering silently.

Judges 4:6–7 — God gave Barak instruction through Deborah. Receive divine strategy.

Isaiah 54:17 — "No weapon that is formed against thee shall prosper…" Even iron chariots cannot override covenant.

2 Corinthians 10:4 — "For the weapons of our warfare are not carnal, but mighty through God…" Systems of bondage must be pulled down spiritually and strategically.

PRAYERS TO CRUSH JABIN

Lord, deliver me from every Jabin spirit. Deliver me from every system, mindset, relationship, structure, and cycle that has been strategically designed to keep me bound. Give me divine wisdom that is greater than oppressive wisdom. Raise up the right voices, the right strategies, and the right partnerships for my freedom. I refuse to normalize bondage. I refuse to accept oppression as my portion. In Jesus' name, amen.

DECLARATIONS

- I declare that every Jabin system is being overthrown.
- Every oppressive strategy is being exposed.
- Every controlling structure is losing power.
- I will not be managed by fear.
- I will not be ruled by intimidation.
- I will not remain under what God has called me to conquer.
- The wisdom of God is greater than the wisdom of the enemy.
- I am coming out. Freedom is my portion.
- Victory is my inheritance.

THE GIANT OF THE PHILISTINES

The Giant of Constant Warfare, Intimidation, Cultural Corruption, and Territorial Opposition

Scriptures: - 1 Samuel 17, Judges 13–16, 2 Samuel 21:15–22

Meaning: The word Philistine is connected to the idea of invaders, migrators, penetrators, or occupiers of territory. Spiritually, the Philistine giant represents anything that invades your life, occupies your territory, opposes your covenant identity, and keeps you trapped in cycles of warfare, intimidation, compromise, pressure, distraction, and spiritual resistance.

The Philistine spirit does not always attack suddenly. Sometimes it wears people down slowly through constant battles, continual resistance, emotional exhaustion, compromise, intimidation, and distractions until they become mentally drained, spiritually numb, emotionally reactive, and disconnected from purpose.

This giant fights people who are called to carry covenant, leadership, influence, worship, creativity, innovation, and spiritual authority.

INTRODUCTION

Before you can fully understand the Philistine giants in the Bible, you must first understand the Philistines themselves. Goliath was not the only giant connected to the Philistines. He was part of a larger culture, system, and bloodline that opposed God's covenant people continuously. The Philistines produced multiple giants throughout Scripture, and each giant represented a different manifestation of warfare, intimidation, pressure, compromise, exhaustion, and opposition.

The Philistines were not occasional enemies of Israel. They were persistent enemies. Throughout Scripture they constantly fought against God's people, battled over territory, attacked worship, challenged leadership, and attempted to influence Israel culturally and spiritually. They understood something powerful: if they could not destroy Israel physically, they would try to corrupt them spiritually and weaken them mentally, emotionally, and culturally.

This is why understanding the Philistines matters. The Philistine giant is not just one battle. It is a spirit of continual warfare, intimidation, compromise, distraction, and resistance designed to wear down people who carry covenant, purpose, creativity, leadership, worship, and Kingdom authority.

THE PHILISTINE GIANTS

The Philistines produced many of the giants found throughout Scripture. Goliath was not the only giant. Second Samuel 21:15–22 reveals several Philistine giants connected to Goliath's bloodline, each representing different dimensions of warfare.

Goliath, whose name is connected to exile, exposure, and uncovering, represents intimidation, public fear, visible opposition, and psychological warfare. He attacked confidence, courage, authority, and identity.

Ishbi-Benob, whose name is connected to dwelling in high places, represents hidden warfare, exhaustion, and attacks against weary leaders. This giant attacked David when he became faint in battle.

Saph, also called Sippai, whose name is connected to thresholds and doorways, represents repeated warfare, cycles, and battles connected to transition seasons. This giant fights people at doors, gates, and moments of advancement.

Lahmi, the brother of Goliath, whose name is connected to bread and provision, represents attacks against supply, provision, and sustenance.

Another Philistine giant described in Scripture had six fingers on each hand and six toes on each foot. This giant symbolizes distortion, excess, abnormality, perversion, and systems that normalize dysfunction and corruption.

These giants reveal that the Philistine spirit attacks multiple areas of life. It attacks confidence, provision, identity, endurance, transition, leadership, culture, and covenant authority.

CONTEXT

The Philistines appear throughout Scripture as one of Israel's greatest enemies. They fought Israel during the days of Samson, Saul, David, and beyond. They constantly battled over territory, wells, worship, influence, leadership, and covenant identity.

One of the clearest examples of the Philistine spirit is when the Philistines stole the Ark of the Covenant. The Ark represented God's presence, glory, authority, and covenant. The Philistines attempted to capture what was sacred while still living in rebellion themselves.

That is what this giant does. The Philistine spirit wants the benefits of covenant without submission to God. It wants power without purity, influence without obedience, success without surrender, and glory without sacrifice.

This giant creates cultures where people slowly become comfortable with compromise. Convictions weaken, discernment becomes dull, standards lower, and people begin adjusting to dysfunction instead of confronting it.

HOW THIS GIANT OPERATES

The Philistine giant thrives through continual warfare and pressure. It attacks mentally, emotionally, spiritually, relationally, financially, creatively, and culturally.

This giant often operates through constant conflict, intimidation, mockery, fear tactics, competition, jealousy, compromise, seduction, spiritual weariness, delayed battles, identity attacks, territorial warfare, and persistent resistance.

The Philistine giant loves to wear people down. It wants people tired, distracted, emotionally reactive, spiritually inconsistent, and mentally exhausted.

This giant especially attacks worshippers, leaders, creatives, pioneers, innovators, and covenant carriers because those people shift atmospheres and move culture.

The Philistine spirit hates people who carry vision and covenant authority.

LIFE APPLICATION

The Philistine giant still operates today. Many people experience continual warfare where it feels like the moment one battle ends, another begins. There is constant pressure, constant resistance, and continual opposition.

This giant often manifests through intimidation. Like Goliath standing before Israel, it uses fear, noise, threats, and emotional pressure to make people feel smaller than they are. It wants people to magnify the battle instead of magnifying God.

This giant also works through compromise and cultural blending. Over time, people start normalizing what God called them to separate from. Convictions weaken. Standards lower. Discernment becomes dull. People begin adjusting to dysfunction instead of confronting it.

The Philistine giant also attacks identity. People dealing with this spirit often struggle with insecurity, comparison, competition, fear of failure, fear of visibility, and feeling like they constantly have to prove themselves.

This giant creates environments filled with strife, confusion, manipulation, jealousy, control, and tension. Peace becomes difficult to maintain.

The Philistine giant also fights creativity. Many creatives experience cycles where every time they try to build, produce, launch, write, create, or move forward, intense resistance suddenly appears.

Instead of focusing on purpose, people become battle focused. Instead of building vision, they spend all their energy recovering from warfare. Over time, this giant erodes confidence, peace, discernment, spiritual sensitivity, endurance, and emotional stability.

WHAT THIS GIANT DOES TO PEOPLE

The Philistine giant slowly erodes confidence, peace, spiritual sensitivity, and endurance. It creates survival mode. People stop dreaming. Stop building. Stop trusting. Stop creating.

Stop resting. Stop believing.

This giant causes people to become battle-focused instead of purpose-focused. Instead of building vision, they spend all their energy managing warfare. Instead of producing, they spend all their energy recovering. Instead of advancing, they spend all their energy defending themselves.

Over time, people become emotionally hardened, spiritually fatigued, mentally scattered, and relationally disconnected.

This giant also creates generational warfare patterns where families stay trapped in cycles of conflict, poverty, division, addiction, anger, fear, and instability.

HOW THIS GIANT ATTACKS LEADERS AND MINISTERS

The Philistine spirit attacks leaders publicly because public fear spreads quickly. It attacks through criticism, pressure, visibility, overwhelming responsibility, public scrutiny, emotional exhaustion, fear of failure, and decision fatigue.

The enemy wants leaders discouraged and silent because when leaders lose courage, communities lose momentum.

This giant attacks ministers through burnout, betrayal, hidden discouragement, isolation, emotional weariness, warfare after obedience, criticism after sacrifice, and constant demands.

Many ministers are fighting giants while smiling publicly. Many are pouring into others while running empty privately.

HOW THIS GIANT ATTACKS CREATIVES

The Philistine spirit hates creativity because creativity shapes culture. Music shapes culture. Film shapes culture. Art shapes culture. Stories shape culture.

If the enemy can silence the creative, he can influence the culture.

This giant attacks creatives through fear of visibility, insecurity, comparison, inconsistency, pressure to perform, self-sabotage, creative exhaustion, delayed execution, and intimidation by larger platforms.

Many creatives are gifted publicly but tormented privately. The enemy wants creatives so battle focused that they stop building.

SIGNS YOU MAY BE DEALING WITH THE PHILISTINE GIANT

One major sign is constant warfare in every area of life. It feels like the moment one battle ends, another begins.

Another sign is intimidation. Fear, pressure, threats, criticism, and emotional warfare make people feel smaller than they truly are.

Another sign is spiritual exhaustion. You love God, but you feel drained mentally, emotionally, and spiritually.

Another sign is compromise. Convictions weaken, standards lower, and discernment becomes dull.

Another sign is cycles of resistance. Every attempt to move forward is met with unusual opposition, delays, confusion, or pressure.

This giant also manifests through comparison, insecurity, jealousy, competition, manipulation, tension, and environments where peace becomes difficult to maintain.

HOW TO CRUSH THE PHILISTINE GIANT

The Philistine giant cannot be defeated through intimidation, fear, compromise, or fleshly striving. It must be crushed through covenant identity, spiritual authority, consistency, discernment, and complete dependence on God.

David defeated Goliath because he understood covenant. While everyone else saw a giant, David saw an uncircumcised Philistine, someone outside covenant. David understood: "What I carry is greater than what I face."

That is the first key to crushing this giant: You must stop measuring yourself against the battle and start measuring the battle against God.

The second key is refusing intimidation. Goliath used noise, threats, fear, and public humiliation. Many people lose battles mentally before they ever fight physically. The Philistine giant wants you afraid to move, afraid to obey, afraid to launch, afraid to confront, afraid to heal, afraid to grow, and afraid to become who God called you to be. You crush this giant by moving forward anyway.

The third key is protecting your spiritual environment. The Philistine spirit thrives in compromised atmospheres. You must guard what enters your spirit through relationships, conversations, entertainment, environments, and influences. Some battles continue because people are feeding the very thing they are praying against.

The fourth key is consistency. The Philistine giant loves inconsistency because inconsistency weakens spiritual stamina. You cannot war one day and disappear the next. Prayer must become consistent. Worship must become consistent. Discipline must become consistent. Healing must become consistent. Small daily obedience crushes large generational giants.

The fifth key is reclaiming territory. Throughout Scripture, the Philistines constantly fought over wells, land, cities, and territory. Spiritually, many people have surrendered territory: their peace, their confidence, their joy, their creativity, their purity, their identity, their family, their discipline, their purpose.

To crush this giant, you must take your territory back. Take your mind back. Take your prayer life back. Take your peace back.

Take your creativity back. Take your discipline back. Take your family back. Take your worship back.

The sixth key is endurance. The Philistine giant often fights through prolonged warfare. Some battles are not won overnight. You must learn how to stand when battles continue longer than expected. Galatians 6:9 reminds us: "Let us not be weary in well doing: for in due season, we shall reap, if we faint not."

The seventh key is understanding spiritual authority. David did not defeat Goliath with Saul's armor. He defeated him with what God had already developed in him privately. Many people are trying to fight public giants with borrowed identities. You crush the Philistine giant by becoming secure in who God created you to be.

SCRIPTURES FOR CRUSHING THE PHILISTINE GIANT

1 Samuel 17:45, Isaiah 54:17, Romans 8:37, 2 Corinthians 10:4–5, Ephesians 6:10–18, Psalm 144:1, Galatians 6:9, Joshua 1:9, Philippians 1:28

PRAYERS TO CRUSH THE PHILISTINE GIANT

Father, in the name of Jesus, expose every Philistine spirit operating against my life, mind, purpose, family, creativity, calling, and covenant identity. Every spirit of intimidation, compromise, fear, exhaustion, warfare, distraction, and resistance must break now in Jesus' name.

Strengthen me where I have become weary. Heal me where warfare has wounded me. Restore my confidence, restore my discernment, restore my peace, and restore my spiritual stamina.

I will not surrender territory You assigned to me. I will not bow to intimidation. I will not compromise under pressure. I declare that every giant standing against my purpose shall fall.

Like David, teach my hands to war and my heart to trust You fully. In Jesus' name, amen.

DECLARATIONS

- I will not be intimidated. I will not compromise. I will not surrender my territory. I will not allow warfare to make me forget who I am.
- I am called, chosen, equipped, and empowered by God.
- Every Philistine giant opposing my purpose shall fall.
- I will recover what was lost. I will rebuild what was broken. I will reclaim my peace, creativity, worship, confidence, discipline, and purpose.
- I will walk in covenant authority, strength, endurance, and victory.

THE GIANT OF GOLIATH

The Giant of Intimidation, Fear, Public Pressure, and Opposition

Scripture: 1 Samuel 17

Meaning: The name Goliath is connected to the ideas of exposure, exile, and uncovering. Spiritually, Goliath represents intimidation, public fear, visible opposition, psychological warfare, and anything designed to make people feel overwhelmed before the battle even begins.

Goliath was designed to be seen. His size, his armor, his weapons, and his presentation were all built to intimidate. Everything about him was meant to magnify fear.

This is why intimidation often operates through visibility. The enemy wants people so focused on the size of the opposition that they forget the size of the God they serve.

Goliath's goal was never simply to win a battle. His goal was to create surrender before the battle started.

INTRODUCTION

Goliath was not just a giant. He was a system of intimidation standing between God's people and victory. He was a Philistine giant whose presence represented warfare, fear, opposition, and public intimidation. Before David ever fought Goliath physically, Israel had already been fighting him mentally. For forty days, Goliath stood before the armies of Israel morning and evening taunting them, intimidating them, and challenging their identity.

What is remarkable is that for forty days Goliath never laid a finger on anyone. He never swung a sword. He never threw a spear. He never physically attacked Israel. His greatest weapon was not his size. His greatest weapon was his voice. He used words. He used threats. He used intimidation. He used fear. He used repetition.

Every morning and every evening he appeared and released the same message. Day after day, his words created an atmosphere of fear until an entire army forgot who they were.

That is how intimidation works. The enemy keeps talking until fear sounds like truth. He keeps presenting pressure until people begin doubting their authority, questioning their assignment, and shrinking back from battles they were called to win. Many people are fighting Goliaths today that have never touched them physically. They are being controlled by words, opinions, criticism, threats, assumptions, insecurities, memories, fears, and internal conversations.

Goliath represents anything that appears too large, too loud, too powerful, or too established for you to confront. He is the giant that stands between you and promise. He is the voice that says, "You are not enough. You are too small. You cannot win this. You do not belong here."

This giant does not simply attack ability. It attacks confidence. It attacks courage. It attacks identity. It attacks authority. It attacks faith.

CONTEXT

First Samuel 17 reveals that Israel stood on one hill while the Philistines stood on another, and between them was the valley. This detail is significant because giants often appear in transitional places. They show up in the space between where you are and where God is taking you.

The locations mentioned in the text are deeply symbolic. Socoh means hedge or enclosure. Azekah means cultivated ground. The Valley of Elah is connected to strength.

This giant appears in the in-between place. You are no longer where you used to be, but you are not fully in possession yet. That valley becomes the place where intimidation attempts to stop movement and progression.

The valley is where many people quit, but it is also where warriors are revealed.

Goliath came from Gath, a name connected to the winepress, a place of crushing, pressure, and squeezing. Pressure does not always mean you are failing. Sometimes pressure means you are being processed. Intimidation is designed to apply pressure until people collapse mentally, emotionally, spiritually, or creatively.

ROOT OF THIS GIANT

The root of Goliath is intimidation, fear-based pressure, and external opposition. Goliath thrives on making people feel smaller than what God created them to be.

This giant attacks through fear, public pressure, criticism, comparison, insecurity, overwhelming situations, and visible resistance. It magnifies obstacles and minimizes identity.

Goliath wants people to become more conscious of the battle than the covenant. He wants them talking more about the giant than about God. He wants them studying the problem instead of remembering the promise.

HOW THIS GIANT OPERATES

Goliath did not just show up quietly. He presented himself publicly. First Samuel 17:4 through 7 describes his height, his armor, and the weight of his weapons in great detail. Everything about him was designed to intimidate before the fight even started.

Presentation can intimidate, but presentation does not equal anointing.

Modern intimidation often comes through polished presentations, influence, visibility, status, large followings, public approval, and systems that appear too powerful to challenge. The enemy wants people so focused on what others carry that they forget what God placed inside of them.

Intimidation always attacks authority before it attacks ability. Before the enemy attacks your hands, he attacks your confidence. Before he attacks your performance, he attacks your perception. Before he attacks your assignment, he attacks your identity.

LIFE APPLICATION

Goliath still appears today through loud opposition, public pressure, fear of failure, fear of confrontation, criticism, insecurity, comparison, and overwhelming situations that seem impossible to overcome.

This giant manifests through systems designed to discourage people from moving forward. It appears through environments where fear is louder than faith and pressure becomes stronger than peace.

Many people know what God called them to do but remain stuck because intimidation convinced them they were not qualified, prepared, worthy, or capable. Goliath is anything standing in front of destiny screaming, "You cannot cross."

For some people Goliath looks like debt. For others it looks like trauma. For others it looks like rejection. For others it looks like a diagnosis. For others it looks like criticism. For others it looks like an impossible assignment. The form changes, but the spirit remains the same.

SIGNS YOU ARE DEALING WITH GOLIATH

One of the clearest signs you are dealing with Goliath is that you feel intimidated by something that has not actually touched you yet. You spend more time worrying about what might happen than dealing with what is happening. You find yourself rehearsing failure instead of expecting victory.

Another sign is that you constantly hear negative internal conversations. You know what God said, but another voice keeps arguing with it. You begin questioning your qualifications, your calling, your ability, your purpose, and your future. You become more aware of your weaknesses than God's strength.

Another sign is procrastination. You know what needs to be done, but fear keeps delaying action.

Another sign is comparison. You become so focused on what others have that you forget what God has given you.

Another sign is feeling stuck in the valley between where you are and where you know God is taking you. You are not moving backward, but you are not moving forward either.

Another sign is that criticism affects you more than confirmation. One negative comment carries more weight than ten encouraging words.

Another sign is that you have become battle focused instead of purpose focused. You spend so much energy managing fear that you stop pursuing destiny. When intimidation begins controlling decisions, Goliath is present.

WHAT THIS GIANT LOOKS LIKE IN MINISTRY

In ministry, Goliath often appears as fear of launching, fear of preaching truth, church politics, intimidation from influential people, pressure to compromise, financial pressure, criticism, visible opposition, exhaustion from warfare, fear of public failure, comparison between ministries, feeling disqualified, and pressure to perform instead of obey.

Sometimes Goliath is not a person. Sometimes it is a religious system. Sometimes it is tradition. Sometimes it is the fear of public opinion. Sometimes it is the pressure to maintain image over authenticity.

This giant wants ministers more focused on survival than obedience.

HOW GOLIATH ATTACKS MINISTERS

This giant attacks ministers through burnout, betrayal, emotional exhaustion, constant demands, hidden discouragement, warfare after obedience, criticism after sacrifice, isolation, and pressure to carry everyone else while bleeding privately.

Many ministers are fighting giants while smiling publicly. Many are pouring into others while running empty internally. The enemy understands that if he can emotionally exhaust the leader, he can weaken the people connected to them.

HOW GOLIATH ATTACKS LEADERS

Goliath attacks leaders publicly because public fear spreads quickly. Goliath challenged Israel in front of everyone because intimidation becomes more powerful when it is witnessed collectively.

This giant attacks leaders through pressure, visibility, criticism, heavy responsibility, decision fatigue, fear of failure, fear of disappointing people, public scrutiny, and overwhelming expectations.

The enemy wants leaders exhausted, discouraged, and silent because when leaders lose courage, communities lose momentum.

HOW GOLIATH ATTACKS CREATIVES

Creatives threaten darkness because creatives shape culture. Music shapes culture. Film shapes culture. Art shapes culture. Stories shape culture. If the enemy can silence the creative, he can influence the culture.

This giant attacks creatives through fear of visibility, insecurity, comparison, inconsistency, self-sabotage, creative exhaustion, pressure to perform, delayed execution, and intimidation by larger platforms.

Many creatives are gifted publicly but tormented privately. The enemy wants creatives so battle focused that they stop building.

This giant especially attacks the space between vision and execution, the tension between calling and visibility, and opportunities that stretch confidence beyond comfort.

DAVID'S POSITIONING

David was not even supposed to be there. He was the youngest. He was tending sheep. He was not in the army. Yet First Samuel 17 reveals that David was sent by his father. He was obeying instructions. He was serving.

Your obedience will position you for battles that reveal you. Serving behind the scenes prepares people for public authority. Hidden seasons produce visible strength.

David heard what others ignored. While everyone else heard intimidation, David heard defiance against God. Others heard fear. David heard opportunity. How you hear determines how you respond. The same giant intimidating everybody else may be announcing your next season.

HOW TO CRUSH THIS GIANT

The first key to crushing Goliath is understanding covenant. David saw something nobody else saw. While everyone else saw a giant, David saw an uncircumcised Philistine. David understood covenant.

The second key is using what God already placed in your hands. David did not need Saul's armor because God had already developed him privately.

The third key is speaking before striking. David declared victory before the battle ever ended. Faith spoke before the stone moved.

The fourth key is remembering previous victories. David remembered the lion and the bear. Past victories produced present confidence.

The fifth key is refusing intimidation. You crush this giant by moving forward anyway.

The sixth key is confronting fear directly. David ran toward Goliath while everyone else retreated.

The seventh key is refusing comparison. Stop measuring yourself against the giant and start measuring the giant against God.

Never forget that David defeated Goliath long before the stone ever hit him. The battle was won when David refused to agree with the giant.

PRAYERS CRUSH GOLIATH

Father, in the name of Jesus, I thank You that You have not given me the spirit of fear, but of power, love, and a sound mind. Today I renounce every spirit of intimidation, fear, insecurity, comparison, and opposition that has attempted to stand between me and the promises You have spoken over my life.

Forgive me for every time I magnified the giant more than I magnified You. Forgive me for every time I listened to the voice of fear more than the voice of faith.

Strengthen my heart where intimidation has weakened me. Restore my confidence where criticism has wounded me. Heal the places where fear has delayed my obedience.

Teach me to see as David saw. Help me remember that what I carry is greater than what I face. Give me courage to move forward, wisdom to use what You have already placed in my hands, and faith to confront every giant standing in my path.

I declare that every voice of intimidation, every threat, every lie, every accusation, and every fear loses its power over my life. I will not retreat. I will not surrender. I will not bow to intimidation.

In Jesus' name, amen.

DECLARATIONS

- I will not be intimidated.
- I will not be silenced.
- I will not be restricted.
- I refuse to magnify the giant above my God.
- I am anointed for this battle.
- I am equipped for this assignment.
- I have overcome lions and bears, and I will overcome this giant.
- I will not allow fear to make decisions for me.
- I will not allow criticism to define me.
- I will not allow comparison to distract me.
- I will move forward in faith.
- I will obey God completely.
- I will confront what others avoid.
- I crush intimidation.
- I crush fear.
- I crush comparison.
- I crush opposition.
- And I will walk fully in the purpose, authority, influence, and destiny God has ordained for my life.

THE SIX FINGERED GIANT

The Abnormal and Excessive Warfare Giant

Scriptures: 2 Samuel 21:20–21, 1 Chronicles 20:6–7

Meaning: This giant represents abnormal warfare, excessive pressure, intensified attacks, irregular patterns, multiplied opposition, and overwhelming situations. This is the giant that makes you ask, "Why is everything happening at once?" It attacks your ability to process clearly. It overloads your emotions. It exhausts your capacity. It creates confusion and makes you feel outnumbered.

The enemy will often exaggerate the battle in an attempt to magnify fear. The significance of the extra fingers and toes is important. Hands represent work, function, production, and execution. Feet represent movement, direction, stability, and territory. This giant had excess in both. In other words, this giant attacks both your productivity and your movement. It wants your hands overwhelmed, your movement disrupted, and your focus divided.

CONTEXT

There are some battles in life that feel familiar. You recognize the pattern. You know where the pressure is coming from. You understand the source of the attack. But then there are other battles that feel excessive, unusual, abnormal, and overwhelming all at once. They do not follow normal patterns. They feel intensified. Multiplied. Irregular. This is the kind of warfare represented by the six fingered giant.

The Bible says in 2 Samuel 21:20, "And there was yet a battle in Gath…" Immediately we see something important again: "there was yet a battle." This matters because it reminds us that warfare is often progressive. One battle ends, and another begins. One season closes, and another challenge rises. Sometimes just when you think you have overcome one thing, another thing appears standing in front of you.

But this battle was different because this giant was different. The Scripture describes him as "...a man of great stature, that had on every hand six fingers, and on every foot six toes, four and twenty in number..." The Bible could have simply called him a giant, but instead it specifically highlights his abnormality. Why? Because details matter.

This giant was excessive. Unusual. Different. Some battles are abnormal because they are designed to overwhelm you.

ROOT OF THIS GIANT

The root of this giant is overload, excess, confusion, pressure, fatigue, scattered focus, and lack of boundaries. It operates where there is no order. It thrives where there is no rest. It gains strength where everything feels urgent, everything feels heavy, and everything feels like it must be handled at once.

This giant thrives in environments without boundaries. It grows when people confuse busyness with obedience, pressure with purpose, and constant availability with assignment.

FOR CREATIVES

This giant attacks creatives heavily because creatives often carry multiple responsibilities at once. This looks like creative burnout, emotional exhaustion, too many assignments, too many expectations, mental overload, and pressure from every direction. You are creating, serving, leading, building, producing, organizing, helping everyone else, and carrying vision all at the same time. Eventually, you begin to feel overloaded.

Creatives must pay close attention to this giant because creativity requires clarity, peace, rhythm, and space. When your mind is cluttered, your creativity becomes strained. When your emotions are overloaded, your creativity becomes heavy. When your body is exhausted and your spirit is depleted, your gift can still function, but it will not flow with the same purity, power, and precision.

WHERE THIS GIANT SHOWS UP

The Bible says this battle took place in Gath. Gath matters because it was also connected to Goliath and was considered a Philistine stronghold. The name Gath means "winepress." A winepress is a place of crushing, pressure, squeezing, and extraction.

Some giants attack in seasons of pressure because pressure reveals what is inside of you. This giant shows up when pressure increases, demands increase, and expectations increase. Everything about this giant was "more." Extra fingers. Extra toes. Extra pressure. Extra intensity. Extra overload. The enemy uses excess to create intimidation. Too many responsibilities. Too many battles. Too many problems happening simultaneously.

This is the "everything at once" giant.

Yet despite how abnormal this giant looked, the Bible says he still fell.

In 2 Samuel 21:21, the Scripture says, "...Jonathan the son of Shimea the brother of David slew him." Jonathan's name means "Yahweh has given." That is powerful because before the battle even began, provision for victory had already been supplied.

God has already supplied what you need for abnormal warfare.

WHAT THIS GIANT DOES

This giant uses confusion, excess, distraction, pressure, fatigue, and overload because if the enemy can overwhelm you, he can interrupt movement. And when movement stops, momentum slows. Purpose delays. Productivity decreases. Assignments remain unfinished.

This giant also attacks mentally. It creates scattered thinking, mental fatigue, emotional exhaustion, indecisiveness, and distraction. You begin overthinking, procrastinating, emotionally reacting, shutting down, and losing focus. Overwhelm is often a weapon of distraction.

SPEED, ACCELERATION, & MOMENTUM

Momentum matters. But before we fully understand momentum, we must understand speed, acceleration, and momentum because this giant attacks all three. It attacks your ability to move, your ability to increase movement, and your ability to sustain movement.

Speed is how fast something is moving. Speed creates movement. But speed alone is not enough. You can move quickly and still be moving in the wrong direction. You can be busy and still not be productive. You can be active and still not be aligned.

Speed without direction creates exhaustion.

Acceleration is the increase of speed over time. This is when opportunities multiply, assignments expand, and visibility increases. Things begin happening faster. But acceleration without structure becomes dangerous. Many creatives pray for acceleration but are not prepared for the pressure that comes with it.

Acceleration without structure becomes overload.

Momentum is sustained movement. It is the force that keeps something moving once it has already started. Speed gets you moving. Acceleration increases your pace. But momentum helps you continue. Momentum is movement with rhythm, force, consistency, and sustainability.

This reminds me of traveling through the airport. You can desire to get to the destination. You can have the ticket. You can be packed and ready. But there are still things that determine the ease and speed of your movement. One of those things is having the right documentation. When you have a KTN, a Known Traveler Number, your movement changes because your identity has already been verified. It does not eliminate process, but it changes how you move through the process.

Spiritually, many creatives want acceleration without verification. They want speed without structure. They want movement without systems. But documentation determines access. Spiritually, your documentation is identity, consecration, clarity, instruction, and obedience. When those things are established, you move differently. You move with authority, clarity, and less friction.

Acceleration is dangerous when identity has not been verified.

SIGNS YOU MAY BE DEALING WITH THIS GIANT

You may be dealing with this giant when everything feels like it is happening at once. You feel pressure from every side. You are emotionally overloaded, mentally scattered, spiritually tired, and physically exhausted. You may notice that you are overthinking, procrastinating, shutting down, reacting emotionally, or losing focus.

You may also be dealing with this giant when your hands feel overwhelmed and your movement feels disrupted. You are working, producing, creating, serving, helping, leading, and carrying responsibility, but your momentum is slowing down. You feel busy but not fruitful. Active but not aligned. Pressured but not productive.

Another sign is when you begin losing rhythm. You start strong, but you struggle to sustain. You begin projects, but you do not finish them. You receive opportunities, but you feel too overwhelmed to steward them well. You want movement, but your mind is cluttered. You want acceleration, but you do not have structure.

For creatives, this giant often shows up as burnout, creative fatigue, emotional exhaustion, too many assignments, too many expectations, and pressure from every direction. You may feel like everyone needs something from you, but you have little left to give.

One of the clearest signs is when boundaries are missing. Everything has access to you. Every need feels like your responsibility. Every opportunity feels like your assignment. Every demand feels urgent. This is how the abnormal and excessive warfare giant gains ground.

PROPHETIC INSIGHT

This giant wants you scattered, overwhelmed, unstable, and exhausted. But God wants you focused, anchored, productive, and at peace. The abnormality of the battle does not change the outcome.

No matter how excessive it looks, no matter how unusual it feels, and no matter how many things seem to be happening simultaneously, this giant can still fall.

Some giants are designed to intimidate you through excess. But remember greater pressure often means greater promise and every abnormal giant can still be crushed.

FOR MINISTRY & LEADERSHIP

This giant also attacks heavily in ministry and leadership because leaders often carry pressure from multiple directions at the same time. Leaders are responsible for vision, people, systems, decisions, growth, stewardship, counseling, correction, administration, and spiritual covering all while still trying to maintain their own emotional, spiritual, and mental health.

This giant thrives where leaders feel like they must carry everything themselves.

In ministry, this giant often looks like constant emergencies, emotional exhaustion, decision fatigue, burnout, mental overload pressure from people, spiritual exhaustion, compassion fatigue overcommitment, lack of rest, trying to meet everyone's expectations constantly solving problems, and carrying the emotional weight of other people's pain.

This giant convinces leaders that slowing down is weakness and that rest means failure. It creates pressure to always produce, always respond, always fix, always lead, and always be available. But even Jesus stepped away from crowds.

Many leaders are drowning privately while functioning publicly. They continue preaching while exhausted, serving while depleted, helping while hurting, and leading while emotionally overloaded. Over time, this giant causes leaders to lose clarity, lose rhythm, lose peace, and eventually lose momentum.

This giant also attacks leaders through scattered focus. Too many meetings. Too many demands. Too many voices. Too many responsibilities. Too many expectations. Leaders begin reacting instead of leading intentionally. Instead of moving strategically, they move emotionally and urgently. This is dangerous because urgency and assignment are not always the same thing.

This giant also creates unhealthy leadership habits. Leaders begin believing: "If I don't do it, it won't get done.", "Everything depends on me." "I cannot slow down." "I cannot trust anyone else with this." But that mindset eventually creates collapse.

Moses dealt with this in Exodus 18 when Jethro told him that the way he was leading was unsustainable. Jethro told Moses, "Thou wilt surely wear away…" because he was attempting to carry alone what was meant to be distributed.

Anointing does not remove the need for structure. Calling does not remove the need for support. Leadership without boundaries eventually becomes self-destruction.

This giant especially attacks visionary leaders and creatives in ministry because vision naturally attracts responsibility. But just because something needs attention does not mean you are assigned to carry it personally.

Delegation is not weakness. Systems are not weakness. Rest is not weakness. Boundaries are not weakness. They are wisdom.

Jesus often withdrew to pray because even He understood the necessity of spiritual replenishment. If Jesus needed moments away from the crowd, leaders must understand they cannot constantly pour out without being refilled.

This giant wants leaders overwhelmed so they become ineffective, emotionally unstable, spiritually drained, mentally scattered, and eventually discouraged.

Because if the enemy can exhaust the leader, he can affect the people connected to the leader.

This is why protecting your peace, your focus, your health, your rest, and your time is not selfish. It is stewardship. Healthy leaders lead better. Rested leaders hear better. Focused leaders move better.

And leaders who learn how to manage pressure properly are able to sustain momentum without destroying themselves in the process.

HOW TO CRUSH THIS GIANT

So how do you crush this giant?

You cannot panic when things look different. Abnormal does not mean unbeatable. Different does not mean defeat. Unexpected does not mean unauthorized. Isaiah 41:10 says, "Fear thou not; for I am with thee…" You cannot allow unusual warfare to create unusual fear. Panic magnifies problems, but prayer magnifies God.

You must simplify the battle. This giant wants everything to feel urgent at the same time. But everything is not equally important. Some things are assignments, and some things are distractions. Victory often begins with simplifying, prioritizing, and slowing down. You defeat overload with focus.

Creatives especially must understand this because many creatives attempt to carry too much simultaneously. They want to answer every call, solve every problem, launch every idea, help every person, and fulfill every request. That is not always anointing. Sometimes it is simply overload.

Focus is warfare. You must create boundaries. Boundaries are not walls to keep people out. Boundaries are systems that protect what God placed within you. Boundaries protect your peace, your creativity, your mental capacity, your time, and your assignment.

Not every opportunity is an assignment. Not every demand deserves access.

Proverbs 4:23 says, "Keep thy heart with all diligence; for out of it are the issues of life." To "keep" means to guard. Guarding your heart is strategy. Guarding your peace is strategy. Many creatives are overwhelmed because they have mistaken constant accessibility for purpose.

Access without honor eventually becomes exploitation.

You must return to God's instructions. When warfare becomes abnormal, the answer is not more activity. The answer is instruction. Isaiah 26:3 says, "Thou wilt keep him in perfect peace, whose mind is stayed on thee…" Peace stabilizes the mind, and a stable mind defeats confusion. Clarity crushes confusion.

You must rest before you break. This giant loves exhaustion. Rest is not weakness. Rest is strategy. Jesus told His disciples in Mark 6:31, "Come ye yourselves apart… and rest a while…" In Exodus 33:14, God says, "My presence shall go with thee, and I will give thee rest."

One of the greatest examples of this is Elijah in 1 Kings 19. Elijah was exhausted, emotionally drained, discouraged, and ready to give up. God did not first give him a sermon. God gave him food. God gave him sleep. Then God told him, "The journey is too great for thee."

Sometimes you are not weak because you lack faith. Sometimes you are weak because you need rest.

Rest is more mental than physical. Many people sit down physically while still exhausted mentally because their minds never stop striving. Real rest is when your soul stops wrestling. Real rest is when your mind settles enough to trust God again.

For creatives, rest restores rhythm. Creativity flows better from peace than pressure. You cannot create clearly when your mind is cluttered or your emotions are overloaded.

You must stop trying to do everything alone. This giant feeds on isolation. Many creatives believe everything depends on them, but that mentality eventually produces burnout. Healthy support systems matter. Accountability matters. Community matters. Delegation matters.

Exodus 18 records Jethro telling Moses that what he was doing was not good because he would eventually wear away trying to carry everything alone. Moses was anointed, chosen, and called, but he still needed help.

Delegation protects destiny. You need systems. You need support. You need people. You do not need everyone carrying the entire vision, but you do need people carrying pieces of it. If you carry everything alone, eventually you will drop something important. Overextension is not proof of effectiveness.

Finally, you must protect your momentum. Galatians 6:9 says, "Let us not be weary in well doing…" Momentum is maintained through consistency, discipline, focus, recovery, and obedience.

Consistency defeats complexity.

PRAYER FOR CRUSHING THIS GIANT

Father, in the name of Jesus, I come before You asking You to give me clarity, peace, focus, discipline, and strength. I renounce every spirit of confusion, overload, pressure, excessive warfare, fatigue, distraction, and emotional exhaustion. I refuse to be overwhelmed by what looks abnormal. I refuse to be intimidated by what appears excessive.

Lord, help me simplify what has become complicated. Help me identify what belongs to me and what does not belong to me. Help me create boundaries that protect my peace, my assignment, my creativity, my time, and my capacity.

Teach me how to rest before I break. Teach me how to trust You enough to stop striving. Restore my rhythm. Restore my focus. Restore my strength. Restore my movement. Restore my momentum.

Father, surround me with healthy support, accountability, wisdom, and people who can help carry pieces of the vision. Deliver me from the need to do everything alone. Give me the courage to delegate, the wisdom to build systems, and the discipline to stay aligned with Your instructions.

I declare that I will not be scattered. I will not be overwhelmed. I will not be emotionally consumed. I will not allow abnormal warfare to create abnormal fear. I will walk in clarity, peace, focus, rest, and authority.

In Jesus' name, amen.

DECLARATIONS

- I will not be overwhelmed.
- I will not be consumed by pressure.
- I will not lose momentum.
- I will not allow excess to intimidate me.
- I have clarity.
- I have peace.
- I have strategy.
- I have focus.
- I have discipline.
- I have rest.
- I have support.
- My hands will not be overwhelmed.
- My feet will not be unstable.
- My movement will not be disrupted.
- My productivity will not be destroyed.
- I will protect my peace.
- I will create healthy boundaries.
- I will return to God's instructions.
- I will rest before I break.
- I will not do everything alone.
- I will delegate with wisdom.
- I will protect my momentum.
- Everything assigned to destroy my movement and productivity must fall.
- I will not just survive this season.
- I will overcome it.

ABIM (ABIMELECH)

The Giant of Illegitimate Authority, Selfish Ambition, and Control

Scripture: Judges 9

Meaning: "My father is king."

CONEXT

The giant of Abim, represented by Abimelech in Scripture, is the giant of illegitimate authority, selfish ambition, family betrayal, manipulation, and leadership obtained through human effort rather than divine appointment. Unlike Goliath, Abimelech was not a physical giant. He was a giant in spirit. He represents the destructive force that emerges when a person desires power more than purpose, position more than process, and authority more than accountability.

Abimelech was the son of Gideon, one of Israel's greatest judges. Yet instead of honoring the legacy of his father, he sought to secure influence through violence, manipulation, and self-promotion. After Gideon died, Abimelech convinced his mother's family to support his rise to power. He then murdered his brothers so there would be no competition for the throne. He wanted rulership, but he did not want rivals. He wanted authority, but he did not want accountability.

This giant does not simply desire influence. It desires exclusive control. It is threatened by the success of others. It struggles to celebrate another person's growth because it interprets every gift, opportunity, and promotion as competition.

The spirit of Abim shows up whenever people attempt to force what God has not yet released. It appears when individuals manipulate relationships, leverage connections, use emotional pressure, create division, or employ fear and intimidation to gain influence. It is the spirit that says, "I deserve to be in charge," while refusing the refining process that prepares a person to lead.

Many people battle the Abim giant without realizing it. It can hide beneath confidence, vision, ambition, and leadership. However, underneath the surface is often insecurity, rejection, fear, comparison, and the desperate need to prove worth through accomplishment.

The Abim giant does not simply seek a seat at the table. It wants ownership of the table.

THE ROOT OF ABIM

At its core, the Abim giant is an identity problem. Abimelech's name means "My father is king," yet he spent his life trying to prove his worth through power, control, and position. Many believers do the same thing. They are already chosen. Already loved. Already accepted. Already called. Already sons and daughters of the King. Yet they continue striving for validation through titles, influence, applause, and recognition.

The Abim giant survives wherever identity is uncertain. But when identity becomes secure in God, the giant loses its power. Secure people do not have to compete. Secure people do not have to manipulate. Secure people do not have to dominate. Secure people do not have to control. Secure people can wait. Secure people can celebrate others. Secure people can trust God's timing. Secure people can trust God's promotion.

When identity is settled, ambition becomes purified, leadership becomes healthy, creativity becomes fruitful, and the giant of Abim is crushed.

WHAT THIS GIANT REPRESENTS

The Abim giant represents corrupted leadership and selfish ambition. It is authority without character. It is influence without integrity. It is visibility without maturity.

This giant often causes people to confuse opportunity with calling and platform with purpose. It convinces individuals that being gifted automatically qualifies them to lead. Yet Scripture repeatedly teaches that gifting may open doors, but character determines whether a person can remain in the room.

The Abim giant seeks to replace God's process with human striving. It tells people to seize what God intended them to receive. It encourages self-promotion instead of divine promotion.

Ultimately, this giant is rooted in pride and insecurity working together. Pride says, "I deserve more." Insecurity says, "I am not enough." The Abim giant feeds both.

LIFE APPLICATION

Most people will never commit the acts that Abimelech committed, yet many struggle with the same underlying spirit.

The Abim giant appears whenever we attempt to secure through manipulation what God intended to provide through obedience. It appears when we push doors open that God has not opened, force relationships that God has not ordained, or seek recognition as a substitute for identity.

Many people are not driven by wickedness but by woundedness. Rejection creates a need to be noticed. Abandonment creates a need to prove worth. Insecurity creates a need to control outcomes. Comparison creates a need to compete.

The Abim giant often grows in the soil of unresolved pain. As a result, people begin pursuing significance rather than identity. They become consumed with titles, positions, influence, applause, and recognition. They seek external validation for internal wounds.

The problem is that no title can heal rejection. No promotion can heal insecurity. No platform can heal identity issues. No audience can heal loneliness. The giant of Abim convinces people that success will heal what only God can heal.

SIGNS YOU ARE DEALING WITH THE GIANT OF ABIM

You may be dealing with the Abim giant when you notice the following patterns:

- A constant need to control people or situations.
- Difficulty celebrating the success of others.
- Feeling threatened by gifted individuals.
- Manipulating relationships to gain influence.
- Seeking position more than purpose.
- Using fear, guilt, or pressure to get your way.
- Becoming jealous when others are promoted.
- Building private alliances instead of healthy relationships.
- Resisting accountability.
- Needing recognition to feel valuable.
- Viewing other people's success as your loss.
- Feeling entitled to opportunities rather than prepared for them.

This giant can also manifest through secret conversations, gossip, division, flattery, and strategic relationship-building designed to advance personal agendas. Individuals influenced by this giant often present themselves as helpful while quietly positioning themselves for control.

HOW THE ABIM GIANT ATTACKS LEADERS

The Abim giant is especially dangerous in leadership because leadership naturally involves influence, visibility, authority, and responsibility.

This giant whispers lies such as:

- Protect your position.
- Don't trust anyone.
- They're trying to take your place.
- Nobody can do it like you.
- You must control everything.
- If you empower them, they may replace you.

When leaders listen to these lies, they begin operating from fear rather than faith. Instead of developing leaders, they collect followers. Instead of empowering others, they control others. Instead of mentoring successors, they eliminate perceived threats. Instead of building teams, they build dependence. Instead of creating healthy organizations, they create unhealthy systems centered around themselves.

The Abim giant is often behind church splits, ministry conflicts, territorial behavior, succession problems, burnout, and leadership isolation.

A leader under the influence of this giant may become defensive when challenged, resistant to correction, unwilling to delegate, intimidated by gifted people, and obsessed with maintaining control. Ironically, the more they seek control, the more isolated they become.

HOW LEADERS CRUSH THE GIANT OF ABIM

Leaders crush the Abim giant by remembering that leadership is stewardship, not ownership. The ministry belongs to God. The church belongs to God. The vision belongs to God. The people belong to God.

Healthy leaders understand that their responsibility is not to make people dependent upon them but to develop people who can thrive beyond them.

Leaders must intentionally practice delegation, mentorship, accountability, succession planning, team development, and shared leadership.

Every time a leader celebrates another person's growth, they weaken the power of Abim. Every time they empower someone else, they dismantle the giant. Every time they choose humility over control, they crush its influence. The strongest leaders are not those who build the largest following. The strongest leaders are those who raise the most leaders.

HOW THE ABIM GIANT ATTACKS CREATIVES

The Abim giant frequently targets creatives because creatives often operate in environments where visibility, recognition, and influence are highly valued. Authors, artists, musicians, speakers, entrepreneurs, content creators, actors, designers, visionaries, and innovators are especially vulnerable to comparison.

This giant whispers:

- Why are they succeeding and not you?
- Your work is better than theirs.
- You deserve more recognition.
- You should have more followers.

- You should be further along by now.
- Why wasn't that opportunity given to you?

Over time, comparison steals joy. Instead of creating from purpose, people begin creating from competition. Instead of serving their audience, they begin chasing applause. Instead of honoring their assignment, they become distracted by someone else's platform.

The Abim giant wants creatives to become obsessed with visibility while neglecting character. It wants them to pursue influence while abandoning authenticity. It wants them to build a brand while neglecting their soul.

HOW CREATIVES CRUSH THE ABIM GIANT

Creatives crush this giant by staying rooted in purpose rather than popularity. Your assignment is unique. Your voice is unique. Your journey is unique. Your timing is unique.

God never called creatives to compete with one another. He called them to create. Creatives overcome the Abim giant by intentionally celebrating the success of others. Every time you applaud another creator, you weaken jealousy. Every time you support another person's work, you weaken comparison. Every time you remain faithful to your assignment instead of chasing someone else's platform, you strengthen your identity.

Healthy creatives understand that influence is a byproduct of obedience. Their goal is not fame. Their goal is faithfulness.

HOW TO CRUSH THE ABIM GIANT

You crush the Abim giant by surrendering your ambition to God. Ambition itself is not sinful. God places dreams, desires, and vision within His people. The problem occurs when ambition becomes fueled by insecurity, rejection, pride, jealousy, or the need for validation.

Philippians 2 teaches believers to do nothing through selfish ambition or vain conceit but to walk in humility and honor others above themselves.

You crush this giant by refusing to manipulate your way into what God has not assigned. If God called you, you do not need to scheme. If God sent you, you do not need to sabotage. If God appointed you, you do not need to destroy others to secure your position.

You also crush this giant by embracing process. David was anointed long before he was crowned. Joseph dreamed long before he ruled. Moses spent years in the wilderness before leading Israel. Jesus spent decades preparing for a ministry that lasted only a few years.

Process protects the promise. Process develops character. Process reveals motives. Process prepares people for what promotion requires. You further crush this giant by celebrating others, practicing gratitude, embracing accountability, and allowing God to heal the wounds that create the need for control.

Most importantly, you crush the Abim giant through repentance. Not surface repentance. Deep repentance. The kind that prays:

"Lord, purify my motives.", "Lord, heal my insecurities.", "Lord, remove the need to control.", "Lord, deliver me from selfish ambition."

"Lord, make me safe for leadership."

PRAYERS FOR CRUSHING THE ABIM GIANT

Prayer for Humility

Father, in the name of Jesus, reveal any area of pride, selfish ambition, control, manipulation, or insecurity operating in my life. Help me to see myself honestly and to surrender every unhealthy motive to You. Teach me to walk in humility, serve with purity, and trust Your timing. Remove every desire to force doors open that You have not opened. Let my life be marked by obedience rather than self-promotion. In Jesus' name, Amen.

Prayer for Leaders

Lord, make me a leader who develops people rather than controls them. Deliver me from territorial thinking, insecurity, fear, and comparison. Help me celebrate the gifts of others and create opportunities for them to grow. Teach me to lead as a steward and not an owner. Let my leadership bring freedom, health, growth, and multiplication. In Jesus' name, Amen.

Prayer for Creatives

Father, protect my heart from comparison, jealousy, and the need for validation. Help me remain faithful to my unique assignment. Teach me to create from purpose rather than competition. Let my creativity glorify You rather than feed my ego. Keep me focused on obedience rather than applause and faithfulness rather than fame. In Jesus' name, Amen.

DECLARATIONS

- I will not manipulate what God has already ordained.
- God's timing is perfect concerning my life.
- I do not need to force what God has promised.
- I celebrate the success of others without comparison or jealousy.
- My identity is rooted in Christ and not in titles, positions, or recognition.
- I am secure in who God created me to be.
- I will lead with humility, integrity, and wisdom.
- I will create from purpose and not from competition.
- God is healing every wound that fuels insecurity and control.
- I trust God's promotion more than my own striving.
- I will not build my kingdom. I will advance God's Kingdom.
- The giant of selfish ambition, manipulation, control, and illegitimate authority is crushed in my life.
- I walk in humility, freedom, obedience, and divine purpose.

Key Scripture - James 4:10

"Humble yourselves in the sight of the Lord, and He shall lift you up."

The Abim giant says, "Lift yourself." God says, "Humble yourself, and I will lift you." One pathway produces temporary influence. The other produces lasting impact.

GIANT OF THE AVIM

The Giant of Distortion, Ruin, Confusion, and Identity Displacement

Scripture: Deuteronomy 2:23

Meaning: Wanderers, invaders, those associated with displacement, vulnerability, instability, and the loss of territory.

CONTEXT

Deuteronomy 2:23

"And the Avims which dwelt in Hazerim, even unto Azzah, the Caphtorims, which came forth out of Caphtor, destroyed them, and dwelt in their stead."

The mention of the Avim in Scripture appears brief, almost insignificant, tucked away within a historical account of nations and territories. Yet, as is often the case in the Bible, a seemingly minor detail reveals a major spiritual principle. The Avim were a people who occupied villages and settlements near Gaza. They lived in the land, built in the land, and existed in the land, yet they ultimately lost the land. Another people came, overpowered them, displaced them, and occupied what once belonged to them.

This is what makes the Giant of the Avim so dangerous. Unlike Goliath, who stood openly in a valley and challenged Israel with intimidation, the Avim giant often works quietly. It is not always seen in a dramatic confrontation. Instead, it operates through erosion rather than explosion. It slowly weakens foundations, disrupts stability, and creates conditions where people lose what they should have been able to maintain. This giant is not merely about losing territory; it is about losing the ability to sustain territory.

Many people spend years praying for open doors, opportunities, relationships, influence, financial breakthrough, ministry growth, emotional healing, or business success. Yet receiving something and maintaining something are two different challenges. Many people know how to obtain blessings but never learn how to steward them. They know how to enter a season but do not know how to remain established in it. The Giant of the Avim attacks maintenance. It attacks sustainability. It attacks longevity. It attacks consistency. It attacks a person's ability to remain rooted long enough to flourish.

The tragedy of the Avim is not simply that they were invaded. The tragedy is that they became vulnerable to invasion. Their story raises a powerful question for every believer: What areas of my life have become vulnerable? What territory has God entrusted to me that I am failing to protect? What blessings have I received that I have not properly stewarded?

The Avim giant appears whenever people repeatedly lose ground they once possessed. It shows up when peace is constantly interrupted by chaos. It shows up when relationships repeatedly collapse. It shows up when finances never seem stable. It shows up when emotional healing is continually sabotaged by old wounds. It shows up when ministries never gain traction. It shows up when gifted people constantly find themselves rebuilding instead of advancing.

At its core, this giant represents displacement. It represents the painful experience of being removed from a place where you should have been flourishing. Sometimes that displacement is physical, but more often it is emotional, spiritual, relational, or mental. A person can own a home and still feel displaced. They can sit in church and still feel disconnected. They can hold a leadership title and still feel unsettled. They can achieve success and still feel insecure.

The Avim giant creates an internal condition of instability. It convinces people they can never fully settle, never fully trust, never fully rest, and never fully establish roots. It produces a constant sense of vulnerability that keeps people living in survival mode rather than walking in confidence and faith.

REVELATION

One of the greatest misconceptions in spiritual warfare is the belief that every giant arrives with obvious hostility. Some giants announce themselves loudly. Others work quietly beneath the surface. Some giants attack through direct confrontation. Others attack through gradual deterioration.

The Giant of the Avim belongs to the second category.

This giant does not always seek to destroy you immediately. Instead, it seeks to weaken your ability to remain established. It attacks consistency. It attacks stability. It attacks structure. It attacks discipline. It attacks healthy boundaries. It attacks anything that helps you stay rooted.

The enemy understands that a person who remains planted will eventually become fruitful. A believer who stays rooted in God's Word will grow. A leader who remains consistent will influence others. A visionary who refuses to quit will eventually build something significant. Therefore, the enemy often focuses less on preventing growth and more on creating instability.

The Avim giant works through cycles. Every time momentum begins to build, disruption appears. Every time trust begins to grow, betrayal emerges. Every time healing begins, an old wound resurfaces. Every time progress is made, chaos arrives to interrupt the process.

Over time, repeated disruption produces something dangerous: an expectation of disruption.

People who have lived under the influence of this giant begin anticipating failure before success arrives. They expect relationships to end. They expect opportunities to disappear. They expect disappointment. They expect betrayal. They expect instability because instability has become familiar.

This is why the Avim giant often creates emotional homelessness. A person may physically have a home, but internally they feel unsettled. They never feel safe. They never feel secure. They never feel established. They carry a subconscious belief that something is always about to go wrong.

The enemy loves this condition because unstable people are easier to distract, easier to discourage, and easier to manipulate. When stability disappears, clarity often disappears with it.

WHAT THE AVIM GIANT LOOKS LIKE

The Giant of the Avim rarely announces itself through one dramatic event. More often, it reveals itself through patterns. It is seen in recurring cycles that keep a person from becoming firmly established in life and purpose.

This giant creates environments where consistency becomes difficult. It causes people to constantly rebuild rather than advance. Instead of moving from strength to strength, they move from crisis to crisis. They become experts at recovery but never experience sustainability.

People under the influence of this giant often feel as though they are living on shifting sand. Every time they gain traction, something destabilizes them. Every time they begin to feel secure, circumstances change. Every time they begin trusting the process, another disruption appears.

The result is a life characterized by uncertainty rather than confidence. The Avim giant commonly manifests through:

- Constant disruption and interruption
- Repeated cycles of loss
- Difficulty maintaining progress
- Emotional instability
- Chronic inconsistency
- Fear of commitment
- Fear of permanence
- Self-sabotage during healthy seasons
- Relationship instability
- Financial instability
- Ministry instability
- Difficulty finishing what was started
- Living in survival mode
- Persistent feelings of vulnerability
- Internal restlessness even during seasons of peace

What makes this giant especially deceptive is that many people mistake its symptoms for personality traits. They say, "That's just how I am." They describe themselves as restless, inconsistent, noncommittal, or constantly changing. In reality, some of these behaviors may be evidence of a deeper spiritual and emotional battle.

The Avim giant thrives when instability becomes normalized. The longer chaos remains present, the more familiar it feels. Eventually, people stop fighting for stability because they no longer believe stability is possible. That is exactly what this giant wants.

SIGNS YOU MAY BE DEALING WITH THE AVIM GIANT

1. You constantly feel uprooted. Even in safe environments, your mind remains on alert. You struggle to relax because you are expecting disruption.

2. You sabotage stability. When things finally become healthy, peaceful, or structured, you unconsciously create chaos because dysfunction feels more familiar than peace.

3. You live in survival mode. You struggle to plan long term because life has taught you that things can collapse at any moment.

4. You struggle with consistency. You start things but have difficulty maintaining them because instability has trained your mind to expect interruption.

5. You fear attachment. You avoid fully connecting to people, places, or assignments because deep down you fear loss, abandonment, or displacement.

6. You constantly feel invaded emotionally, mentally, spiritually, or relationally. Boundaries become weak and peace becomes difficult to maintain.

HOW THE AVIM GIANT ATTACKS LEADERS

One of the reasons the Giant of the Avim is so dangerous is because it specifically targets builders. Leadership is fundamentally about stewardship. Whether a person is leading a church, a business, a ministry, a family, a nonprofit organization, or a movement, leadership is the responsibility of managing, protecting, developing, and multiplying territory that has been entrusted by God.

This is why the Giant of the Avim often targets leaders with unusual intensity. The enemy understands a principle that many leaders overlook: if he can destabilize the leader, he can often destabilize everyone connected to the leader. A leader's health impacts the health of the organization. A leader's clarity impacts the clarity of the team. A leader's consistency impacts the consistency of the culture.

The Giant of the Avim rarely attacks leaders by taking away their calling. Instead, it attacks their ability to sustain what God has given them. It attacks their stability. It attacks their endurance. It attacks their capacity to remain rooted when pressure increases.

Many leaders under the influence of this giant find themselves constantly rebuilding. Instead of moving from one level of growth to another, they spend much of their time repairing damage, managing conflict, correcting avoidable mistakes, or recovering from repeated setbacks. Every time momentum begins to build, another disruption appears. Every time progress becomes visible, a new crisis emerges.

One of the primary ways the Avim giant attacks leaders is through inconsistency. Leaders may find themselves constantly changing direction, revising plans, abandoning initiatives prematurely, or reacting emotionally to circumstances. Vision becomes difficult to sustain because instability creates uncertainty.

The Avim giant frequently isolates leaders as well. Many leaders begin carrying burdens alone because they feel responsible for everyone around them. They stop seeking counsel. They stop asking for help. They stop allowing trusted people to speak into their lives.

Isolation becomes dangerous because instability grows where accountability is absent.

Another manifestation of this giant is reactive leadership. Instead of leading from vision, leaders begin leading from crisis. Every decision becomes a reaction to the latest problem. Every meeting becomes an attempt to put out another fire. Every conversation centers on damage control rather than growth.

The tragedy is that many leaders begin accepting this cycle as normal. Yet God never intended leaders to operate from perpetual instability. Throughout Scripture, effective leadership is associated with wisdom, order, discernment, and consistency. The Kingdom of God advances through structure and stewardship, not through confusion and chaos.

Signs the Avim Giant May Be Operating in a Leader

1. Constantly changing direction without clear discernment.
2. Repeatedly rebuilding systems that continually collapse.
3. Living in crisis-management mode.
4. Difficulty maintaining healthy teams.
5. Emotional exhaustion and decision fatigue.
6. Frequent feelings of being overwhelmed.
7. Fear of long-term commitments.
8. Isolation from accountability and wise counsel.
9. Losing momentum every time growth begins.
10. Feeling responsible for everything while trusting no one.

HOW THE AVIM GIANT ATTACKS CREATIVES

Creatives often experience the Giant of the Avim differently than leaders, but the underlying objective remains the same. While leaders are frequently attacked through organizational instability, creatives are often attacked through emotional, mental, and creative instability.

The enemy understands the power of creativity because creativity reflects the nature of God. God is a Creator, and every creative person carries the capacity to produce something that did not previously exist. Whether through writing, music, art, entrepreneurship, innovation, ministry, teaching, speaking, or design, creatives have the ability to bring vision into reality.

Because creativity possesses such transformative power, the Avim giant works diligently to keep creatives unsettled. It seeks to disrupt focus, interrupt momentum, and create cycles of inconsistency. Many gifted individuals are not struggling because they lack talent. They are struggling because they lack stability.

Many creatives live with a constant feeling of starting over. They have notebooks filled with ideas, journals filled with concepts, computers filled with unfinished projects, and dreams that remain undeveloped. Inspiration comes easily, but completion becomes difficult.

The Avim giant frequently attacks creatives through distraction. New ideas continually compete with existing assignments. Every opportunity appears exciting. Every possibility seems urgent. Rather than focusing on completion, creatives become trapped in a cycle of perpetual beginnings.

Comparison is another weapon commonly used against creatives. The giant convinces them to measure their journey against someone else's success. Comparison produces insecurity, and insecurity often leads to inconsistency.

The Avim giant also attacks through perfectionism. Some creatives delay completion because they believe their work must be flawless before it can be released. What appears to be excellence is often fear disguised as refinement.

Creative exhaustion is another common manifestation of this giant. Creatives pour out ideas, solutions, strategies, content, encouragement, innovation, and inspiration. However, when they fail to replenish themselves, they become depleted. Burnout follows. Confidence declines. Motivation weakens.

One of the greatest deceptions of the Avim giant is convincing creatives that inspiration alone is sufficient. Inspiration may begin the assignment, but discipline finishes it. The most productive creatives understand that consistency matters more than occasional bursts of motivation.

SIGNS AVIM IS OPERATING IN THE CREATIVE

1. Constantly starting projects without finishing them.
2. Frequent creative burnout.
3. Chronic procrastination rooted in fear.
4. Perfectionism that prevents completion.
5. Constant comparison to others.
6. Difficulty maintaining focus.
7. Emotional highs followed by emotional crashes.
8. Abandoning ideas too early.
9. Fear of visibility and exposure.
10. Feeling scattered despite being gifted.
11. Losing confidence every time progress begins.
12. Living in inspiration without developing discipline.

HOW TO CRUSH THE AVIM GIANT

The first step in crushing the Avim giant is establishing spiritual stability. You cannot overcome instability while remaining disconnected from God. Stability begins with consistency in prayer, consistency in the Word, consistency in worship, and consistency in obedience.

Psalm 1:3 - "And he shall be like a tree planted by the rivers of water..."

Trees that flourish are planted. Roots matter. Stability matters. Consistency matters. A constantly uprooted tree cannot flourish properly.

The second step is breaking agreement with survival mode. Many people have survived for so long that survival became their identity. They no longer know how to live in peace because they have become accustomed to pressure. But survival is not the same as thriving.

Jeremiah 29:11 - "For I know the thoughts that I think toward you... thoughts of peace, and not of evil..."

You must renew your mind to believe that stability is possible. Peace is possible. Healthy relationships are possible. Consistency is possible. Emotional healing is possible.

The third step is building healthy boundaries.

Proverbs 4:23 - "Keep thy heart with all diligence..."

Protect your atmosphere. Protect your peace. Protect your focus. Protect your assignment. Boundaries are not rejection; boundaries are wisdom.

The fourth step is creating systems and structure.

1 Corinthians 14:40

"Let all things be done decently and in order."

This giant hates order because order exposes chaos. Structure creates sustainability. Systems protect progress. Whether you are a leader, creative, entrepreneur, parent, pastor, counselor, or visionary, systems help preserve what God has entrusted to you.

The fifth step is healing from displacement trauma. Many people are reacting to present situations through the lens of past instability. Old abandonment still affects current relationships. Old betrayal still affects current trust. Old rejection still affects current confidence. Healing requires honesty. You cannot heal what you refuse to confront.

Finally, leaders must become rooted and creatives must become disciplined. Leaders crush this giant through stewardship. Creatives crush this giant through consistency. Both crush this giant by remaining planted long enough for fruit to appear.

THE PROPHETIC WARNING OF THE AVIM

The Avim were displaced because they could not maintain their territory. The warning for every believer is clear: what God gives must also be stewarded. Territory requires protection. Vision requires discipline. Purpose requires consistency. Influence requires character. Calling requires endurance.

The enemy's goal is not simply to stop you from receiving God's promises. His goal is to keep you from sustaining them. But through prayer, discipline, healing, healthy systems, accountability, and spiritual maturity, the Giant of the Avim can be crushed.

You are not called to live displaced. You are not called to constantly start over. You are not called to spend your life rebuilding what should have been established. You are called to occupy, build, protect, multiply, and remain. You are called to be planted. You are called to be rooted. You are called to be established and what God establishes, no giant has the authority to remove.

PRAYERS TO CRUSH AVIM

Father, in the name of Jesus, expose every area of instability operating in my life. Heal every place where my soul has been uprooted through trauma, abandonment, rejection, betrayal, disappointment, and fear. Deliver me from survival mode. Teach me how to live planted, grounded, disciplined, and established. Strengthen my mind, emotions, relationships, finances, leadership, creativity, and spiritual life. I declare that I will no longer live emotionally displaced. I will not be overtaken by chaos. I will not constantly restart what You have called me to build. I will walk in peace, stability, structure, wisdom, and divine establishment. In Jesus' name, amen.

DECLARATIONS

- I am planted and not uprooted.
- I break agreement with instability and chaos.
- I am emotionally secure and spiritually grounded.
- I will not live in survival mode.
- I will flourish where God has planted me.
- I am consistent, disciplined, focused, and stable.
- I will build and maintain what God has given me.
- I will not constantly start over.
- I am rooted, grounded, and established in God.
- Peace is my portion.
- Stability is my inheritance.

- I will occupy the territory God has given me.
- I will protect what God has entrusted to me.
- I will finish what God has called me to build.

ANAK / ANAKIM

The Giant of Identity

Scripture: Numbers 13:33; Joshua 11:21

Meaning: Long-necked (pride, dominance)

CONTEXT

When the spies entered the Promised Land, they saw giants, the Anakim. But here's what's powerful: the giants didn't speak first; the people spoke about themselves first. "We were like grasshoppers..."

They weren't defeated by the giant; they were defeated by their perception of the giant.

THE ROOT: insecurity, comparison, and agreement with fear.

SIGNS YOU ARE DEALING WITH THE GIANT OF ANAK

The giant of Anak rarely announces itself openly. Instead, it causes people to constantly measure themselves against everyone around them. The spies said: "We were in our own sight as grasshoppers, and so we were in their sight." (Numbers 13:33)

Notice something important. The giants never called them grasshoppers. They called themselves grasshoppers. Anak works by shrinking your identity before you ever face the battle.

You may be dealing with Anak if:

- You constantly compare yourself to others.
- You feel intimidated by successful people.
- You struggle to celebrate other people's victories.
- You talk yourself out of opportunities before trying.
- You feel unqualified even when God has qualified you.

- You discount your gifts while magnifying everyone else's.
- You feel "less than" in rooms where God placed you.
- You assume others are more capable than you.
- You struggle with imposter syndrome.
- You believe God can use others but secretly wonder if He can use you.
- You avoid visibility because you fear criticism.
- You feel small when facing large assignments.
- You compare your beginning to someone else's middle.
- You focus on your weaknesses more than God's strength.

The giant of Anak causes people to spend so much time looking at others that they stop looking at God.

HOW ANAK ATTACKS LEADERS

Leaders often encounter Anak when God begins expanding their influence. The giant whispers:

"Who do you think you are?" "You are not experienced enough." "You are not educated enough." "You are not anointed enough." "Someone else could do this better."

Anak causes leaders to second-guess decisions. It creates leadership paralysis. It causes gifted leaders to remain hidden while less qualified people step forward simply because they possess confidence.

Many leaders are not defeated by a lack of ability. They are defeated by a lack of belief in what God has already placed inside them.

Anak causes leaders to compare ministries, churches, budgets, platforms, attendance, social media numbers, influence, and visibility. Instead of stewarding their assignment, they become distracted by someone else's assignment. Comparison always leads to confusion because God never called you to become someone else. He called you to become you.

HOW ANAK ATTACKS CREATIVES

Creatives battle Anak constantly. Writers compare books. Authors compare sales. Artists compare talent. Singers compare voices. Entrepreneurs compare businesses. Content creators compare followers.

The giant of Anak convinces creatives that what they have created is not enough. It whispers things like "Nobody will read it." "Nobody will buy it." "Nobody will listen." "Somebody already did it better." As a result, books never get published. Songs never get recorded. Businesses never launch. Ideas never leave the notebook.

Dreams die in seed form because comparison convinces people they have nothing valuable to offer. The truth is that God never called creatives to be copies. He called them to be creators. Anak fears originality because originality carries the fingerprint of God.

PROPHETIC INSIGHT

One of the greatest revelations in the story of the Anakim is this: The giants were not the biggest problem. The mindset was. Israel lost forty years because of a perspective problem.

The same giants that caused ten spies to retreat were the same giants Joshua and Caleb believed they could defeat. The difference was not the giant. The difference was vision. The enemy understands that if he can make you see yourself incorrectly, he can stop you without ever touching you.

The spirit of Anak attacks identity because identity determines destiny. When you do not know who you are, you will surrender territory God already gave you. When you know who you are, giants become temporary obstacles rather than permanent barriers.

Prophetically, many people are standing at the edge of promises that God has already approved. The battle is no longer about whether God can do it. The battle is whether you can see yourself doing what God said. God is raising up a generation of Joshua and Caleb believers who refuse to call themselves grasshoppers.

HOW TO CRUSH THE GIANT OF ANAK

Crushing Anak begins with renewing your identity. Stop measuring yourself against people. Start measuring yourself against God's promises. Remember who God says you are.

Speak God's Word over yourself daily. Reject comparison. Celebrate others without diminishing yourself. Focus on your assignment.

Stay connected to people who remind you of your purpose. Refuse self-disqualification. Walk by faith even when you feel inadequate. Most importantly, remember that God never asks whether you are enough. He asks whether He is enough.

PRAYER FOR CRUSHING THE GIANT OF ANAK

Father, in the name of Jesus, I repent for every place where I have compared myself to others and allowed comparison to distort my identity. Forgive me for seeing myself through the lens of fear rather than through the lens of Your promises. I renounce every grasshopper mentality, every lie of inadequacy, insecurity, intimidation, self-rejection, and self-disqualification.

Lord, help me see myself the way You see me. Heal every wound that causes me to feel small. Break every stronghold of comparison and insecurity. Remove every false label that has attached itself to my identity.

Teach me to walk confidently in the assignment You have given me. Help me celebrate the gifts of others while fully embracing the gifts You placed within me. Strengthen my faith to believe that what You have spoken concerning my life shall come to pass.

I declare that I will not surrender territory because of fear. I will not retreat because of intimidation. I will not abandon purpose because of comparison.

I receive the courage of Joshua and Caleb. I choose faith over fear, confidence over insecurity, and truth over deception.

In Jesus' name, Amen.

DECLARATIONS FOR CRUSHING THE GIANT OF ANAK

- I am who God says I am.
- I reject every grasshopper mentality.
- I refuse to compare myself to others.
- I will not shrink to fit into places God called me to lead.
- I am fearfully and wonderfully made.
- God has equipped me for my assignment.
- What God has called me to do; I am capable of doing through Christ.
- I celebrate others without diminishing myself.
- My identity comes from God, not people's opinions.
- I am not disqualified.
- I am not inadequate.
- I am not overlooked by God.
- I carry the gifts, talents, and abilities necessary for my purpose.

- I will possess the territory God has promised me.
- I walk in faith, confidence, boldness, and authority.
- Giants may be large, but my God is greater.
- I am not a grasshopper. I am an heir of God's promises.
- I do not merely defeat giants—I crush them.

REPHAIM

The Stronghold Giant

Scripture: Genesis 14:5; 2 Samuel 5

Meaning: Shades, terrifying ones ancient giants tied to territories, often valleys.

Root: Generational patterns, spiritual heaviness.

Life Application: Cycles in families, "This always happens to me" patterns.

CONTEXT

2 Samuel 5:18–19 "The Philistines came and spread themselves in the valley of Rephaim…"

David had just stepped into kingship. New level, new territory, new authority. And immediately, the giants showed up. But here's

what separates David: 2 Samuel 5:19 "And David inquired of the Lord, saying, Shall I go up…?" David did not move on assumption, emotion, or past experience. He went to God first. You don't defeat strongholds by rushing into battle— you defeat them by going to God first.

A stronghold is: A fortified pattern, a repeated cycle, a deeply rooted way of thinking or living.

2 Corinthians 10:4 "The weapons of our warfare are not carnal, but mighty through God to the pulling down of strongholds."

In military terms, a stronghold is: A fortified place of defense, built to resist attack, designed to hold territory. To protect what is inside, to keep enemies out, to maintain control over a region.

But here's the deeper truth: A stronghold can also work in reverse. A stronghold becomes: A place where the enemy hides, reinforces control, resists removal. A stronghold is not just something you face, it's something that has been fortified over time.

Strongholds are not taken by random attacks, emotional reactions, or one-time effort. They are conquered through strategy, persistence, surrounding and cutting off supply, repeated pressure.

Strategy → Prayer + Instruction, Cutting supply → Starving wrong habits/thoughts, Pressure → Consistency in truth and discipline.

You don't tear down strongholds in a moment; you dismantle them through consistency. Strongholds are not created overnight. They are built over time through repeated behavior, repeated thoughts, repeated experiences, unhealed wounds, and generational patterns. What you repeat, eventually becomes reinforced.

A stronghold is a pattern that has been practiced long enough to feel permanent. "This just runs in my family" "I've always been this way" "No matter what I do, I end up here again" Cycles in relationships, finances, emotional health, and spiritual discipline.

After David won the first battle, the enemy came back again.

2 Samuel 5:22–23 David inquired again. And this time, God gave him a different strategy. You cannot use yesterday's strategy for today's

battle. Go to God first. 2 Samuel 5:19 Always ask: "Should I move?" "How should I move?"

Victory is not in movement, it's in alignment. David didn't just go into battle; He only moved when God said: "I will go with you." You don't defeat strongholds alone. You defeat them with God's presence and power.

You must identify the cycle, interrupt the behavior, replace it with truth. Romans 12:2 "Be transformed by the renewing of your mind..."

Strongholds live in the mind first. Replace lies with scripture, speak truth out loud, journal patterns you see.

2 Samuel 5:24 "When you hear the sound, then move" Timing matters. Instruction matters. Some victories are not about strength; they are about obedience to timing.

This giant shows up as creative cycles (start/stop patterns), inconsistency, emotional highs and lows, and repeating the same mistakes. You create, stop, restart, and repeat. That's not a discipline issue, that's a stronghold.

Strongholds are not permanent; they are patterns waiting to be broken.

SIGNS YOU ARE DEALING WITH THE GIANT OF REPHAIM

The Rephaim are often associated throughout Scripture with ancient giants, lingering strongholds, and territories that remained occupied long after God had promised freedom.

Spiritually, the giant of Rephaim represents strongholds, generational cycles, entrenched patterns, recurring battles, and issues that seem larger than one lifetime.

Unlike some giants that attack suddenly, Rephaim attacks through longevity. It convinces people that because something has existed for a long time, it will always exist.

You may be dealing with the giant of Rephaim if:

- You repeatedly face the same struggles year after year.
- Certain family patterns seem impossible to break.
- You feel trapped in cycles of dysfunction.
- You repeatedly return to old habits after periods of victory.
- You often say, "This is just how my family is."
- You feel hopeless about lasting change.
- You battle recurring emotional, spiritual, or relational strongholds.
- You continually revisit wounds you thought were healed.
- You experience repeated patterns of self-sabotage.
- You struggle to maintain breakthrough.
- You feel like you're fighting battles that existed before you were born.
- You constantly feel stuck despite genuine effort.

The giant of Rephaim specializes in convincing people that permanent bondage is normal.

HOW REPHAIM ATTACKS LEADERS

Rephaim often attacks leaders through inherited dysfunction. A leader may inherit unhealthy systems, toxic cultures, unresolved conflicts, financial instability, or deeply rooted organizational problems.

The giant whispers "This has always been this way." "Nothing is going to change." "The previous leaders couldn't fix it." "You might as well learn to live with it."

Rephaim attacks vision. It attacks reform. It attacks transformation. It attempts to convince leaders that maintenance is safer than breakthrough.

Many leaders are not battling a lack of skill. They are battling ancient patterns that resist change. The giant wants leaders to manage strongholds instead of confronting them. It wants leaders to preserve dysfunction rather than dismantle it.

HOW REPHAIM ATTACKS CREATIVES

Creatives often encounter Rephaim through repeated cycles of fear, inconsistency, procrastination, and unfinished assignments.

The giant whispers "You always quit." "You never finish." "You've tried before." "What makes this time different?"

Many creatives are not fighting a lack of talent. They are fighting deeply rooted patterns.

Rephaim attacks momentum. It causes creatives to begin projects with excitement and abandon them before completion. It resurrects old disappointments and previous failures. It convinces gifted individuals that their history predicts their future.

As a result, books remain unwritten. Businesses remain unlaunched. Songs remain unreleased. Dreams remain dormant.

Not because the creative lacks ability, but because the giant continually points them backward instead of forward.

PROPHETIC INSIGHT

One of the most important truths about Rephaim is that many of these giants represented old territories that should have already been conquered. The battle was not always about gaining new ground. Often it was about fully possessing ground that God had already given. Many believers are asking God for new territory while old strongholds still occupy existing territory.

God often begins breakthrough by confronting what has been tolerated. The giant of Rephaim thrives wherever people mistake familiarity for permanence. Just because something has existed for decades does not mean God intends for it to remain.

Just because a family pattern has survived generations does not mean it cannot be broken. Just because a stronghold has occupied territory for years does not mean it owns the territory.

The prophetic message of Rephaim is simple:

Long-standing does not mean everlasting. The God who delivered yesterday still delivers today. The God who breaks chains still breaks chains. The God who heals generations still heals generations. What has existed for years can be broken in a moment when God's power is applied.

HOW TO CRUSH THE GIANT OF REPHAIM

Crushing Rephaim begins by identifying recurring patterns. Stop normalizing what God wants to heal. Stop excusing what God wants to transform.

Expose cycles. Confront strongholds with truth. Replace inherited beliefs with biblical beliefs. Develop new habits that support freedom. Seek healing where wounds remain unresolved.

Renew your mind through Scripture. Surround yourself with people who support transformation rather than dysfunction. Refuse to allow your history to define your future. Most importantly, remember that cycles only continue when they remain unchallenged.

Every giant can survive being ignored. No giant survives being confronted.

PRAYER FOR CRUSHING THE GIANT OF REPHAIM

Father, in the name of Jesus, I come before You acknowledging that You are the God of freedom, deliverance, and breakthrough. Today I surrender every recurring battle, every stronghold, every generational cycle, and every pattern that has attempted to remain in my life.

Lord, reveal every area where I have accepted bondage as normal. Expose every lie that says change is impossible. Break every agreement I have made with limitation, defeat, and hopelessness.

I renounce every cycle of fear, failure, dysfunction, self-sabotage, and spiritual stagnation. I declare that what has been passed down does not have to continue through me.

Heal every wound that feeds unhealthy patterns. Restore every area that has been damaged by long-standing strongholds. Give me wisdom to recognize cycles and courage to confront them.

I receive Your freedom. I receive Your healing. I receive Your power to overcome every entrenched battle.

By faith, I declare that old chains are breaking, old patterns are ending, and new seasons are beginning.

In Jesus' name, Amen.

DECLARATIONS FOR CRUSHING THE GIANT OF REPHAIM

- I break agreement with every unhealthy cycle.
- My history does not determine my destiny.
- I am free from every stronghold Christ has defeated.
- What has existed for years can be broken by God's power.
- Generational patterns stop with me.
- I will not normalize bondage.
- I will not tolerate what God wants to heal.

- I possess every territory God has assigned to me.
- I am being transformed by the renewing of my mind.
- Old habits are losing their power over my life.
- I walk in freedom, healing, and restoration.
- I am not trapped by my past.
- I am not defined by family dysfunction.
- God is creating new patterns in my life.
- Strongholds are falling.
- Chains are breaking.
- Freedom is my inheritance.
- I do not merely defeat giants, I crush them.

EMIM

The Fear Giant

Scripture: Deuteronomy 2:10–11

Meaning: Dreaded ones / feared people

Root: Fear, intimidation, anticipation of negative outcomes. The Emim were a people known for one defining characteristic: They were feared. They were described as great, numerous, and tall, similar to the Anakim.

Life Application: Fear of failure, fear of starting, fear of stepping into new territory.

CONTEXT

The Emim were not necessarily the most powerful giants. But they were the most feared. This means something critical: Their greatest weapon was not strength. It was perception and reputation. They were defeated in the mind of the people before they were ever faced in reality.

Deuteronomy 2:1–3 "You have compassed this mountain long enough…"

Israel had been going in circles, stuck in a pattern, moving, but not progressing. And fear was a part of that cycle. Fear will keep you moving, but never advancing.

But then God interrupted the cycle. He gave them specific instructions. Deuteronomy 2:3 "Turn you northward" Change direction. Shift posture. Move differently. Breaking fear starts with changing direction.

Deuteronomy 2:4–5 "You are to pass through the territory of your relatives, the descendants of Esau, who live in Seir. They will be afraid of you…" The people you were afraid of, were actually afraid of you.

Seir Meaning: Rough, hairy, rugged place. Represents hard places, difficult seasons, terrain that requires endurance.

God's instruction: "Do not provoke them" "Do not fight them" "I have already given that land to Esau" Not every battle is yours. God told them: Don't fight, don't strive, don't take what I didn't assign to you. Instead: Pay what you owe, honor boundaries, move forward in obedience.

Deuteronomy 2:9 (Moab) "Do not harass Moab. I have given to the descendants of Lot…"

Moab Meaning: "From father" (connected to Lot's lineage). Represents things that came from a place of mixture, things God allowed but didn't assign to you. God is not giving you what belongs to someone else. He is giving you what belongs to you.

Fear will make you fight wrong battles. Fear causes unnecessary fights, misdirected energy, frustration. If you don't know your assignment you will fight everything.

SIGNS YOU ARE DEALING WITH THE GIANT OF EMIM

The giant of Emim thrives on fear. Unlike some giants that attack through deception, pride, or comparison, Emim attacks through intimidation and dread. It specializes in creating worst-case scenarios. It magnifies problems. It exaggerates obstacles. It causes people to anticipate disaster before anything has happened.

The giant of Emim does not need a real threat to operate. Sometimes it works through imagined threats. Sometimes it works through possibilities. Sometimes it works through memories. Its goal is to keep people trapped in fear long before a battle ever begins.

You may be dealing with the giant of Emim if:

- You constantly expect the worst.
- You struggle with excessive worry.
- You feel overwhelmed by uncertainty.
- You avoid opportunities because of fear.
- You frequently imagine negative outcomes.
- You delay important decisions because you fear failure.
- You experience panic when facing change.
- You struggle to trust God during difficult seasons.
- You replay fearful scenarios in your mind.
- You avoid risks even when God is leading you forward.
- You feel emotionally exhausted from carrying fear.
- You struggle to rest because your mind never stops worrying.
- You magnify problems and minimize God's promises.
- You spend more time thinking about what could go wrong than what God could do.

The giant of Emim seeks to paralyze progress through fear.

HOW EMIM ATTACKS LEADERS

Leaders often face Emim when God begins expanding their assignment.

The giant whispers "What if you fail?" "What if people leave?" "What if you make the wrong decision?" "What if the vision does not work?" "What if you lose everything?"

Emim causes leaders to become overly cautious. It creates indecision. It causes leaders to delay necessary action. It keeps vision trapped in planning stages. Many leaders are not defeated by opposition. They are defeated by the fear of opposition.

The giant of Emim convinces leaders to prepare endlessly while never moving forward. It causes them to focus on potential threats rather than God's promises. Fearful leaders often become reactive rather than visionary. Instead of leading from faith, they lead from survival.

HOW EMIM ATTACKS CREATIVES

Creatives frequently battle Emim because creativity requires vulnerability. Every book, song, business, painting, sermon, or idea requires stepping into uncertainty.

The giant whispers: "What if nobody likes it?" "What if nobody buys it?" "What if they criticize you?" "What if you embarrass yourself?" "What if you fail publicly?"

Emim causes creatives to overedit, overthink, overanalyze, and overprepare. Projects remain unfinished. Ideas remain hidden. Dreams remain buried.

The giant is not afraid of your talent. It is afraid of your obedience. Fear has killed more dreams than failure ever could. The graveyard of unrealized potential is filled with people who listened to Emim.

PROPHETIC INSIGHT

The greatest weapon of Emim is not danger. It is anticipation. Most of the battles people fear never actually happen. Yet they suffer emotionally as though they already have.

Fear causes people to experience tomorrow's problems with today's strength. That is why fear is exhausting. The enemy understands that if he can keep you afraid of the future, he can rob you of your present.

Throughout Scripture, whenever God called someone into greater purpose, He repeatedly said:

"Fear not."

"Be strong and courageous."

"Do not be afraid."

Why? Because fear is one of the greatest enemies of destiny.

The giant of Emim attempts to convince you that the size of the threat is greater than the size of your God. But faith reminds us that God has never lost a battle. Prophetically, many people are standing on the edge of breakthrough, but fear is attempting to make them retreat.

It is time to stop consulting your fears. Stop negotiating with intimidation. Stop bowing to possibilities that have not happened. The future belongs to those who move forward in faith.

HOW TO CRUSH THE GIANT OF EMIM

Crushing Emim begins by confronting fear with truth. Identify the fears controlling your decisions. Challenge fearful thoughts with Scripture. Replace worst-case thinking with God-focused thinking. Pray instead of worrying.

Act in faith even when fear is present. Stop feeding fear through constant negativity. Surround yourself with faith-filled voices. Focus on God's character rather than uncertain circumstances.

Remember that courage is not the absence of fear. Courage is moving forward despite fear. Every time you obey God while afraid, fear loses power. Every time you step forward, the giant shrinks. Most importantly, remember that fear predicts defeat while faith expects victory.

PRAYER FOR CRUSHING THE GIANT OF EMIM

Father, in the name of Jesus, I come before You surrendering every fear, worry, anxiety, dread, and intimidation that has attempted to control my life. I repent for every time I allowed fear to speak louder than Your promises.

Lord, reveal every area where fear has influenced my decisions. Break every stronghold of worry, panic, dread, and emotional torment. I renounce every agreement with fear and choose to trust You completely.

Help me to see situations through the eyes of faith rather than through the lens of fear. Strengthen my confidence in Your power, Your protection, and Your faithfulness. Teach me to move forward even when uncertainty remains.

I declare that fear will no longer dictate my future. I choose courage. I choose faith. I choose obedience.

Thank You for being my refuge, my fortress, and my defender. I place every concern into Your hands and receive Your peace.

In Jesus' name, Amen.

DECLARATIONS FOR CRUSHING THE GIANT OF EMIM

- I refuse to be controlled by fear.
- God has not given me a spirit of fear.
- I walk by faith and not by sight.
- Fear will not determine my decisions.
- I trust God's promises above my circumstances.
- My future is in God's hands.
- I am strong and courageous.
- God is fighting for me.

- I will not retreat from my assignment.
- I reject worry and embrace peace.
- I will not magnify problems above God's power.
- Every fearful thought must submit to the truth of God's Word.
- I am protected by the presence of God.
- I move forward in confidence and faith.
- Fear loses power every time I obey God.
- I am more than a conqueror through Christ.
- Giants may create fear, but God creates victory.
- I do not merely defeat giants, I crush them.

ZAMZUMMIM

The Mental Giant

Scripture: Deuteronomy 2:20.

Meaning: Plotters / murmurers / schemers.

Root: Thought patterns, internal, dialogue, negative agreement within.

Life Application: Overthinking, anxiety, mental loops, negative self-talk.: The Zamzummim were considered a people great, numerous, and tall like the Anakim. But their distinguishing characteristic is in their name: Plotters, murmurers.

CONTEXT

The Zamzummim didn't just operate externally. They operated through internal influence. Their name literally suggests constant talking, internal murmuring, ongoing mental noise. This is the giant that doesn't fight your hands, it fights your mind. Unlike other giants, this one lives inside of you. It builds internal arguments, imaginary scenarios, false conclusions.

2 Corinthians 10:5: "Casting down imaginations..." That word "imaginations" means arguments, reasoning, internal conversations. Some of your biggest battles are conversations you're having with yourself.

This giant grows through repeated thoughts, unchallenged beliefs, fear-based assumptions, past experiences. What you think repeatedly becomes what you believe. What you believe becomes how you live.

If you don't interrupt the thought, you will eventually live it. "

How it shows up in real life": "What if this doesn't work?" "What if I fail?" "What if they don't like it?" "Maybe I'm not ready…" Endless internal dialogue.

For creatives: over-editing, overthinking, starting but not finishing, second-guessing everything. You can't move forward if your mind keeps pulling you back.

Zamzummim also means murmurers. This connects directly to Israel in the wilderness. Numbers 14:2: "All the children of Israel murmured…" They spoke doubt, fear, complaint. And what they said internally became their reality externally. Your internal dialogue will eventually become your external outcome.

SIGNS YOU ARE DEALING WITH THE GIANT OF ZAMZUMMIM

The giant of Zamzummim attacks the battlefield of the mind. The name Zamzummim is connected to murmuring, plotting, scheming, and mental noise. Spiritually, this giant represents mental warfare, confusion, overthinking, obsessive thoughts, tormenting thought patterns, double-mindedness, and internal arguments.

Unlike Goliath, who shouts from the outside, Zamzummim speaks from the inside. It is the giant that keeps conversations going in your head long after everyone else has moved on. It causes people to replay failures. It causes people to relive conversations. It causes people to imagine arguments that have not happened. It creates mental exhaustion through constant internal activity.

You may be dealing with the giant of Zamzummim if:

- You constantly overthink situations.
- You replay conversations repeatedly.
- You struggle to shut your mind off.
- You battle racing thoughts.
- You have difficulty making decisions.
- You constantly second-guess yourself.
- You create scenarios that never happen.
- You struggle with mental peace.
- You have difficulty focusing.
- You feel mentally exhausted even when physically rested.
- You frequently talk yourself out of opportunities.
- You analyze situations to the point of paralysis.
- You struggle with double-mindedness.
- You find yourself trapped in cycles of mental torment.
- You battle confusion regarding decisions God has already made clear.

The giant of Zamzummim seeks to exhaust people mentally before they ever engage the battle physically.

HOW ZAMZUMMIM ATTACKS LEADERS

Leaders are often vulnerable to Zamzummim because leadership requires decision-making. The result is hesitation. The result is indecision. The result is leadership fatigue.

Many leaders are not overwhelmed by the size of their assignment. They are overwhelmed by the noise in their minds.

Zamzummim causes leaders to continually revisit decisions that have already been made. It causes them to seek excessive confirmation. It creates mental clutter that interferes with clarity.

A confused leader often becomes an ineffective leader. The giant knows that if it can cloud your thinking, it can delay your movement.

HOW ZAMZUMMIM ATTACKS CREATIVES

Creatives often encounter Zamzummim through perfectionism and over analysis. The giant whispers: "It is not ready." "It is not good enough." "Keep revising." "Keep tweaking." "Keep changing it."

Before long, months become years. Projects remain unfinished. Books remain unpublished. Businesses remain unlaunched. Songs remain unreleased. Ideas remain trapped inside notebooks.

The giant convinces creatives that thinking about the work is the same as doing the work. But creativity requires movement. Perfectionism is often fear wearing a disguise. The giant of Zamzummim knows that an unfinished masterpiece impacts no one.

PROPHETIC INSIGHT

One of the enemy's favorite strategies is mental occupation. Throughout Scripture, God repeatedly addressed the mind because He understood that battles are often won or lost before they ever appear externally.

The battlefield is rarely the circumstance. The battlefield is interpretation. The enemy knows he cannot always stop God's promises. But he can attempt to exhaust God's people while they wait for them.

Many people are fighting battles that exist nowhere except inside their thoughts. They are arguing with conversations that never occurred. They are fearing events that never happened. They are carrying burdens God never assigned.

The Lord is calling His people back into mental rest. There is a difference between thinking and torment. There is a difference between wisdom and worry. There is a difference between discernment and suspicion.

Prophetically, God is restoring clarity to many who have lived under mental noise. The fog is lifting. Confusion is breaking. Mental clutter is being removed. The voice of God is becoming clearer than the voice of fear.

HOW TO CRUSH THE GIANT OF ZAMZUMMIM

Crushing Zamzummim begins by guarding your mind.

Learn to identify thoughts that agree with God and thoughts that oppose Him.

Take every thought captive. Replace lies with Scripture. Limit unnecessary mental clutter. Reduce exposure to voices that create confusion. Practice prayer instead of mental rehearsal. Practice trust instead of constant analysis.

Refuse to entertain thoughts that produce fear, confusion, or torment. Make decisions and move forward. Do not worship certainty. Trust God's guidance. Most importantly, remember that clarity often comes through movement. Many answers appear after obedience begins.

Daily strategy: Pause when negative thoughts arise. Ask: "Is this truth or assumption?" Replace it immediately. You are not responsible for every thought, but you are responsible for what you do with it.

Renew your mind daily. Romans 12:2. This is not a one-time event. It is a daily process. Practical: Read the Word daily. Write truth statements. Repeat them consistently.

Control your mouth. Because what you think eventually comes out of your mouth. Proverbs 18:21: "Death and life are in the power of the tongue…" Stop speaking negativity. Speak life intentionally. If you keep saying it, you will eventually see it.

Think on the right things. Philippians 4:8. Think on truth, purity, good report. Daily practice: Redirect your thoughts. Be intentional about focus.

For creatives, this giant is extremely active in creatives. It causes creative paralysis, inconsistency, perfectionism, fear-based delay. You start projects, but don't finish them. Your mind becomes the bottleneck of your assignment.

The battle is not just in what you face, it's in what you think. The giant of Zamzummim wants you trapped in endless contemplation. God wants you walking in confident obedience.

PRAYER FOR CRUSHING THE GIANT OF ZAMZUMMIM

Father, in the name of Jesus, I surrender every anxious thought, every racing thought, every confusing thought, and every mental stronghold that has attempted to occupy my mind. I repent for every time I entertained thoughts that opposed Your truth.

Lord, bring peace where there has been torment. Bring clarity where there has been confusion. Silence every voice that is not Your voice. Break every cycle of overthinking, double-mindedness, fear, and mental exhaustion.

Teach me to recognize Your voice above every other voice. Help me discern truth from deception. Strengthen my mind through Your Word and renew my thinking according to Your promises.

I reject confusion and receive clarity. I reject torment and receive peace. I reject mental chaos and receive the mind of Christ.

Thank You for guarding my thoughts, directing my decisions, and leading me into truth.

In Jesus' name, Amen.

DECLARATIONS

- I have the mind of Christ.
- My thoughts are aligned with God's truth.
- I reject confusion.
- I reject mental torment.
- I reject overthinking and double-mindedness.
- God's peace guards my heart and mind.
- I walk in clarity and wisdom.
- I hear God's voice clearly.
- Fear does not control my thinking.
- I refuse to rehearse negative possibilities.
- My mind is disciplined and focused.
- Every thought must submit to the authority of Christ.
- I choose trust over anxiety.
- I choose obedience over hesitation.
- My mind belongs to God.
- I am mentally strong, spiritually stable, and emotionally healthy.
- God is restoring clarity to my life.
- I do not merely defeat giants, I crush them.

SPECIAL INSIGHT: ZAMZUMMIM AND MENTAL HEALTH

Of all the giants in the land, Zamzummim may be one of the most relevant to modern culture. People are more connected than ever, yet many are mentally exhausted. Information overload. Decision fatigue. Constant notifications. Comparison. Fear. Stress. Unresolved trauma.

All of these create fertile ground for mental noise. Not every mental struggle is demonic. Not every mental struggle is spiritual. Sometimes healing requires prayer, counseling, community, healthy habits, rest, and professional support working together.

However, regardless of the source, God desires wholeness in the mind. The giant of Zamzummim loses power when truth, healing, wisdom, and God's peace work together. A noisy mind cannot hear clearly. A peaceful mind becomes fertile ground for God's direction.

HORITES

The Hidden Giant

Scripture: Deuteronomy 2:12

Meaning: Cave dwellers / those who live in holes.

Root: Hidden issues, buried pain, unaddressed areas.

Life Application: Secret struggles, unhealed wounds, private battles no one sees. Bring things into the light (Luke 8:17), address what's hidden. What you hide grows, what you expose heals.

CONTEXT

The Horites were a people who lived in caves and hidden places. They occupied land before others came in and displaced them.

The Horites didn't fight in open fields. They lived in caves. That means they operated from hidden places, dark spaces, unseen environments. This is the giant that survives because it stays hidden.

This giant does not always show up publicly. It lives beneath the surface, behind the scenes, in private areas of your life. It hides in unprocessed emotions, trauma, shame, secrets. You can look whole publicly and still be wounded privately.

This giant grows through avoidance, suppression, denial, silence. What you refuse to deal with goes underground. And what goes underground grows stronger over time.

Hidden things don't die; they develop.

HOW THIS GIANT SHOWS UP

Smiling in public but struggling in private, avoiding certain conversations, triggered reactions you don't understand, patterns you can't explain. You don't know why you respond the way you do, but something underneath is driving it.

For creatives, this giant is very active in creatives. It shows up as creating from pain but never healing, using creativity as an escape, avoiding internal work, masking brokenness with gifting. Your gift can cover your wounds, but it can't heal them.

Hidden issues eventually affect decisions, impact relationships, distort perception. And over time, what was hidden becomes evident. Luke 8:17: "Nothing is hidden that will not be made known…" Exposure is not punishment; it's an opportunity for healing.

SIGNS YOU ARE DEALING WITH THE GIANT OF THE HORITES

The Horites are an often-overlooked enemy in Scripture, yet they occupied territory before God's people arrived. Their name is associated with cave dwellers, those who lived hidden in the mountains and underground places.

Spiritually, the giant of the Horites represents hiding, isolation, avoidance, retreat, emotional withdrawal, secrecy, and living beneath what God has called you to become.

While some giants attack openly, Horites operate in hidden places. This giant does not always tell you to quit. It simply tells you to withdraw. It convinces people that hiding is safer than healing. It persuades people to retreat instead of advancing.

The giant of the Horites thrives wherever people live in emotional, spiritual, or relational caves. You may be dealing with the giant of the Horites if:

- You isolate yourself when facing problems.
- You avoid difficult conversations.
- You withdraw when you feel hurt.
- You struggle to trust others.
- You hide your gifts and talents.
- You fear being seen.
- You resist vulnerability.
- You avoid leadership opportunities.
- You frequently retreat from relationships.
- You struggle with secrecy.
- You avoid accountability.
- You spend more time hiding than healing.
- You allow fear of rejection to keep you disconnected.
- You remain emotionally unavailable.
- You stay in familiar places even when God is calling you forward.

The giant of the Horites convinces people that safety is found in hiding.

God teaches that freedom is found in bringing things into the light.

HOW THE HORITES ATTACK LEADERS

Leaders often encounter the Horite spirit after disappointment, betrayal, criticism, or burnout.

The giant whispers "Stay to yourself." "Don't trust anybody." "Don't let people get close." "Don't share what you're carrying." "You are safer alone."

As a result, leaders begin leading publicly while suffering privately. They become isolated. Disconnected. Emotionally exhausted. The danger of isolation is that leaders lose perspective.

Many leaders do not fall because they lack gifting. They fall because they lose healthy connection.

The giant of the Horites understands that isolated leaders are vulnerable leaders. It attempts to cut leaders off from accountability, encouragement, correction, and support.

A leader in a cave eventually loses sight of the mountain.

HOW THE HORITES ATTACK CREATIVES

Creatives often encounter Horites through fear of exposure. As a result, creatives remain hidden.

The giant convinces creatives that protection is found in remaining unseen. But hidden gifts cannot change lives. A buried seed never produces a harvest. The enemy knows that what remains hidden cannot fulfill its purpose. The giant of the Horites is not afraid of your potential. It is afraid of your visibility.

PROPHETIC INSIGHT

Throughout Scripture, caves often represented places of transition. David hid in caves. Prophets hid in caves. Elijah hid in a cave. Yet God never intended the cave to become a permanent residence. The cave was a temporary shelter, not a permanent assignment.

Many people are living in places they were only supposed to visit. God may allow seasons of retreat. He may allow seasons of healing. He may allow seasons of preparation. But eventually He calls people back into purpose.

The giant of the Horites attempts to turn temporary refuge into permanent residence.

It convinces people that hiding is wisdom. God says there comes a time to emerge. Prophetically, many people have spent years hiding from pain, rejection, disappointment, failure, and fear.

They are being called out of the cave. Out of isolation. Out of secrecy. Out of fear. Out of self-protection. This is a season of emergence. What has been hidden is coming into the light. What has been buried is coming forth. What has been silenced is finding its voice again.

HOW TO CRUSH THE GIANT OF THE HORITES

Crushing the Horites begins by stepping into the light. Bring hidden struggles before God. Seek accountability. Build healthy relationships. Refuse isolation. Engage community. Confront avoidance.

Address conversations you have been postponing. Allow yourself to be seen. Allow yourself to be known. Allow yourself to heal.

Stop confusing hiding with healing. Stop confusing retreat with recovery. Stop confusing isolation with peace. God did not create you to live in caves. He created you to walk in purpose. Most importantly, remember that healing grows in connection.

Darkness survives in secrecy. Freedom grows in the light.

PRAYER FOR CRUSHING THE GIANT OF THE HORITES

Father, in the name of Jesus, I come before You surrendering every place where I have hidden myself because of fear, pain, disappointment, rejection, or shame. Forgive me for every time I chose isolation instead of healing and secrecy instead of freedom.

Lord, expose every area where I have withdrawn from the life You called me to live. Heal every wound that causes me to retreat. Break every agreement with fear, avoidance, self-protection, and isolation.

Give me courage to step into the light. Help me trust you with the parts of my life I have kept hidden. Surround me with healthy relationships, wise counsel, and people who encourage growth and healing.

Teach me to embrace connection rather than isolation. Teach me to walk in transparency rather than secrecy. Teach me to move forward rather than retreat.

I declare that I am coming out of every cave the enemy tried to make permanent. I am stepping into freedom, healing, purpose, and visibility.

In Jesus' name, Amen.

DECLARATIONS

- I refuse to live in isolation.
- God is bringing me out of every cave.
- I walk in the light and not in secrecy.
- I choose healing over hiding.
- I choose connection over isolation.
- I choose courage over avoidance.
- My gifts will not remain hidden.
- My voice will not remain silent.
- Fear will not keep me confined.
- Shame will not keep me concealed.
- God is restoring healthy relationships in my life.
- I am emerging into purpose.
- I am stepping into visibility.
- I am no longer retreating from my calling.

- What God placed inside me will be revealed.
- Darkness loses power when exposed to light.
- Freedom is my inheritance.
- I do not merely defeat giants, I crush them.

SPECIAL INSIGHT
THE DIFFERENCE BETWEEN HIDING AND HEALING

One of the greatest deceptions of the Horites is convincing people that hiding and healing are the same thing. They are not.

Healing may require solitude. Healing may require rest. Healing may require reflection. But healing eventually moves you toward wholeness, connection, and purpose.

Hiding moves you toward isolation, fear, and stagnation. Healing prepares you to reengage life. Hiding convinces you to avoid it. A season in the cave may be necessary. A life in the cave is not. God is not merely calling people to survive their caves. He is calling them to come out of them.

OG

The Giant of Generational Strongholds

Scripture: Deuteronomy 3:1–11.

Meaning: Massive / long-necked / powerful.

Root: Generational cycles, long-standing patterns, deep-rooted strongholds. Og was the king of Bashan, one of the last remaining giants of the Rephaim. He wasn't just a giant. He represented a system that had been in place for a long time. Deuteronomy 3:11: "Og king of Bashan was the last of the remnant of the giants…" His bed alone was over 13 feet long.

Life Application: "This runs in my family," repeated cycles, patterns that seem bigger than you.

CONTEXT

Just because it's been there a long time doesn't mean it has a right to stay. Deuteronomy 3:1–2 shows that Og came out to fight Israel. He didn't hide. He confronted them directly. And here's what God said: "Do not fear him…" When dealing with generational giants, God doesn't tell you to avoid them. He tells you to confront them.

Bashan means "Fruitful place / fertile land." This is powerful. A giant was sitting on a fruitful place. Generational strongholds often sit on the most fruitful areas of your life, areas like relationships, finances, identity, and purpose. What should produce is being occupied.

For creatives, your creativity is supposed to produce, but cycles may have limited it. Your gift is fruitful, but inconsistency may have sat on it. Your influence is meant to grow, but patterns may have restricted it.

Og means powerful, massive, dominant. It represents something that looks too big to defeat and something that feels established and immovable. This is the giant that says, "This is just how it is."

Before Og, Israel defeated another king, Numbers 21:21–31, King Sihon. Sihon means warrior, storm, uproar, and represents resistance, opposition, and confrontation before possession. Deuteronomy 3:2

says, "Do to him what you did to Sihon…"

God will use past victories as a blueprint for present battles. In other words, you've already done this before, you already have the capacity, and you already know how to win. What you defeated before prepared you for what you're facing now.

For creatives, that last project prepared you, that last challenge trained you, and that last "win" built your confidence.

Deuteronomy 3:3–6 shows that they struck him down, left no survivors, and destroyed everything that opposed them. They didn't manage the giant, they eliminated it. This wasn't partial victory. This was total domination.

Deuteronomy 3:7 shows they took livestock, goods, land, and cities. Victory over giants produces reward. What once belonged to the enemy became theirs. They went from fighting for survival to

walking in abundance. From generational curses to generational blessings, before there were cycles, limitations, and restrictions, but after there was increase, inheritance, and expansion. When you defeat a generational giant, you don't just change your life, you change your legacy.

How it shows up in real life is in the same relationship cycles, the same financial struggles, the same emotional patterns, and the same spiritual inconsistencies. Different people, same results. When patterns repeat, you're not dealing with coincidence, you're dealing with a stronghold.

For creatives, this giant shows up as generational limitations in success, lack of exposure, lack of consistency, and fear of breaking new ground. "No one in my family has done this…" You may be the first, but you won't be the last. Deuteronomy 3:11 shows that his bed was massive. God will allow you to face something big so you can reveal something greater. For creatives, big assignments, big platforms, and big opportunities require big faith.

How to crush generational giants begins with confronting it and not ignoring it. Deuteronomy 3:2 says, "Do not fear him…" Avoidance preserves cycles, but confrontation breaks them. You must identify the pattern, what keeps repeating?

For creatives, where do you stop, where do you quit, and where do you hesitate? You must make a different decision, choose differently, and respond differently.

Romans 12:2 shows that transformation breaks repetition. You must partner with God, "I have already delivered him…" You are not fighting for victory; you are fighting from it.

You must stay consistent through daily discipline and repeated obedience. Consistency is how you evict what has been established.

Generational curses do not just appear randomly. They are established through patterns of behavior, repeated disobedience, unresolved issues, and spiritual agreements. Exodus 20:5 says, "Visiting the iniquity of the fathers upon the children unto the third and fourth generation..."

This does not mean God is punishing children for their parents' sins. It means patterns that are not broken become cycles that are inherited. Job 5:6 says, "Affliction does not come from the dust..." Cycles do not happen without a cause. There is always a root, there is always a door, and there is always a pattern.

Generational cycles form through repetition. What is practiced becomes patterned, what is patterned becomes normalized, and what is normalized becomes inherited. A generational curse is simply a pattern that went unchallenged long enough to become a system.

The Bible gives clear examples of these patterns. In Abraham, Isaac, and Jacob, there was a pattern of deception. Genesis 12:13, Genesis 20:2, and Genesis 26:7 show that Abraham lied and said Sarah was his sister, and Isaac did the same thing with Rebekah. What Abraham tolerated, Isaac repeated. This was not coincidence; this was a pattern.

In Genesis 11:31, Terah started the journey but stopped in Haran and never reached the destination God intended. Then in Genesis 12:1, God told Abraham, "Get out... to a land that I will show you..."

Abraham had to continue what his father did not complete. What one generation delays, the next generation must decide to finish.

These patterns also showed up in family dysfunction, favoritism, and division. Isaac favored Esau, Rebekah favored Jacob, and Jacob's sons repeated dysfunction. When patterns are not addressed, they evolve, but they do not disappear.

Just like curses can pass down, blessings can too. Genesis 17:7 says, "I will establish my covenant between me and thee and thy seed after thee…" Psalm 112:2 says, "His seed shall be mighty upon earth…" What you build in obedience, your children inherit as advantage.

Abraham's obedience established a covenant that Isaac inherited, Jacob inherited, and Israel became a nation. One man's obedience shifted generations.

David's faithfulness positioned Solomon. In 1 Kings 3:11–13, Solomon walked into wealth, wisdom, and influence. You can fight battles your children will never have to fight. Breaking generational curses and releasing blessings requires intentional action. You must confront the pattern, because what you do not confront you will continue.

You must change your agreement and stop saying, "This runs in my family." You do not break cycles by accepting them. You must make a different decision and respond differently. Transformation breaks repetition. You must partner with God, because you are not trying to win, you are enforcing victory.

Seed is a critical strategy. Galatians 6:7 says, "Whatsoever a man soweth, that shall he also reap…" Seed is how cycles are broken and new ones are established. A seed introduces something new into an existing system. It disrupts what was and introduces what can be. You do not just stop a cycle; you replace it with a seed.

In Scripture, one seed can shift an entire bloodline. Isaac sowed in famine in Genesis 26:12 and reaped a hundredfold. He introduced abundance in a season of lack. The widow in 1 Kings 17 sowed her last, and the cycle of lack broke. Seeds work the same way naturally and spiritually, financial seeds, time seeds, behavior seeds, and spiritual seeds.

Whatever you sow consistently, you create a future harvest of. If poverty is the pattern, you sow generosity. If inconsistency is the pattern, you sow discipline. If fear is the pattern, you sow faith actions. You do not break cycles by stopping behavior alone, you break them by sowing something different.

Generational curses are broken through confrontation, but generational blessings are established through intentional sowing. I am not just breaking what was, I am building what will be. My obedience becomes inheritance. My decisions become legacy. My seeds become generations.

Og represents what has been sitting on your inheritance, but it has no right to stay. This cycle ends with me. This pattern breaks with me. I will not repeat it. I will not pass it down. I will not agree with it. And everything that belongs to me, I will possess it.

SIGNS YOU ARE DEALING WITH THE GIANT OF OG

Og, king of Bashan, was one of the last remaining giants of the Rephaim. Scripture emphasizes his enormous size, even mentioning his massive iron bedstead (Deuteronomy 3:11).

Spiritually, Og represents strongholds that appear immovable, overwhelming obstacles, intimidation through size, entrenched systems, impossible situations, and battles that seem too large to overcome. Og is the giant that makes people say "This is too big." "This will never change." "This problem is impossible." "This obstacle is larger than me." Unlike some giants that attack through subtle deception, Og attacks through sheer magnitude. He wants you to focus on the size of the problem rather than the size of God.

You may be dealing with the giant of Og if:

- You feel overwhelmed by circumstances.
- You frequently describe your problems as impossible.
- You feel stuck facing obstacles that seem too large to move.
- You struggle to believe breakthrough is possible.
- You constantly focus on what is wrong.
- You become discouraged by how long a battle has lasted.
- You feel intimidated by large challenges.
- You avoid difficult situations because they appear overwhelming.
- You feel powerless against systems or circumstances.
- You often feel defeated before the battle begins.
- You find yourself saying, "Nothing will ever change."
- You struggle to envision victory.
- You magnify obstacles and minimize opportunities.
- You believe the problem is bigger than the promise.

The giant of Og survives by convincing people that size determines outcome.

HOW OG ATTACKS LEADERS

Leaders often encounter Og when God calls them into assignments larger than their resources. The giant whispers "You don't have enough people." "You don't have enough money." "You don't have enough influence." "You don't have enough experience." "The challenge is too big."

Og attempts to intimidate leaders through scale. Large budgets. Large needs. Large problems. Large responsibilities. Large opposition.

The giant wants leaders to become consumed by what they lack rather than what God provides. Many leaders never fail because the challenge was too big. They fail because they became overwhelmed by the appearance of the challenge. Og wants leaders to measure the assignment by their strength. God measures the assignment by His strength.

HOW OG ATTACKS CREATIVES

Creatives frequently encounter Og through overwhelming visions and intimidating goals. The giant whispers "The project is too large." "You'll never finish." "It will take too much work." "You're too late." "There are too many obstacles."

As a result, creatives become overwhelmed before they begin. Books remain unwritten because the manuscript seems too large. Businesses remain unlaunched because the vision feels too complicated. Dreams remain dormant because the process appears overwhelming.

The giant of Og understands that people often abandon what feels impossible. He specializes in creating intimidation through magnitude. The problem is not the size of the vision. The problem is allowing the size of the vision to become larger than faith.

PROPHETIC INSIGHT

One of the most fascinating things about Og is that God addressed him before the battle even started. In Deuteronomy 3:2, God told Moses: "Fear him not." God knew that Og's greatest weapon was not his strength. It was his appearance. His size. His reputation. His intimidation.

Before God discussed strategy, He addressed fear. This reveals an important truth: Many giants lose power the moment fear loses influence.

Prophetically, many people are standing in front of situations that appear larger than anything they have faced before. Large assignments. Large opportunities. Large transitions. Large responsibilities. Large breakthroughs.

The enemy wants them to focus on the size of the obstacle. God wants them to focus on the size of the promise. The battle against Og is never truly about the giant. It is about perspective.

When God says, "Fear not," He is revealing that victory is already available.

HOW TO CRUSH THE GIANT OF OG

Crushing Og begins by changing your focus. Stop measuring the obstacle. Start measuring God's faithfulness. Break large problems into manageable steps. Focus on obedience rather than outcomes.

Refuse intimidation. Remember previous victories. Study what God has already done in your life. Feed your faith instead of your fear. Speak God's promises over impossible situations. Surround yourself with people who strengthen your faith.

Most importantly, remember that God never asks you to carry the assignment alone. The battle belongs to Him. The victory belongs to Him. The outcome belongs to Him.

When God is involved, impossible becomes possible.

PRAYER FOR CRUSHING THE GIANT OF OG

Father, in the name of Jesus, I bring before You every obstacle, challenge, stronghold, and situation that appears larger than my ability to overcome. I confess that there have been moments when I focused more on the size of the problem than on the greatness of Your power.

Today I surrender every intimidating circumstance into Your hands. Break every spirit of fear, discouragement, intimidation, and defeat that has attempted to influence my thinking.

Lord, strengthen my faith. Help me see my battles through Your perspective. Remind me that no giant is larger than You. Remind me that no obstacle can stand against Your promises.

Give me courage to move forward even when the challenge appears overwhelming. Help me trust You one step at a time.

I declare that every giant standing between me and my purpose must bow before the authority of Jesus Christ.

In Jesus' name, Amen.

DECLARATIONS

- My God is greater than every obstacle.
- I refuse to be intimidated by large challenges.
- What seems impossible with man is possible with God.
- I walk by faith and not by sight.
- Fear will not control my decisions.
- God is fighting my battles.
- I will not be overwhelmed.
- I will not retreat from my assignment.
- Every giant must bow before God.
- My faith is greater than my fear.

- God has already prepared victory.
- I possess the territory God has promised me.
- I am equipped for every assignment God gives me.
- No obstacle is bigger than God's power.
- I choose courage over intimidation.
- I choose faith over discouragement.
- I choose obedience over fear.
- I do not merely defeat giant, I crush them.

Og was the king of Bashan, one of the last remaining giants of the Rephaim. He wasn't just a giant. He represented a system that had been in place for a long time. Deuteronomy 3:11: "Og king of Bashan was the last of the remnant of the giants..." His bed alone was over 13 feet long.

SPECIAL INSIGHT: WHEN THE GIANT LOOKS BIGGER THAN YOU

One reason Og is so important is that he represents the moments in life when the challenge truly is bigger than us. Sometimes the diagnosis is bigger than us. Sometimes the debt is bigger than us. Sometimes the grief is bigger than us. Sometimes the responsibility is bigger than us. Sometimes the vision is bigger than us.

That is not failure. That is often exactly where God wants us. God has never required His people to be bigger than the giant. He has only required them to trust the God who is.

The purpose of Og is to teach us that some victories can only happen when we stop trusting ourselves and start trusting God completely. A giant's size is irrelevant when God is involved. The battle was never designed to prove how strong you are. The battle was designed to reveal how strong God is.

SIHON

The Resistance/Blocking Giant

Scripture: Numbers 21:21–31; Deuteronomy 2:24–37.

Meaning: Warrior / tempest / uproar.

Root: Resistance, unnecessary opposition, blocked progress.

Life Application: Doors closing unexpectedly, opposition when trying to move forward, resistance when stepping into new levels. Sihon was the king of the Amorites who stood in the way of Israel's progress. Israel wasn't even trying to fight him at first. They asked for passage. Numbers 21:22: "Let us pass through your land…" But instead of allowing passage, Sihon came out to fight.

CONTEXT

Israel approached Sihon with peace. "Let us pass through…" "We won't touch anything…" "We'll stay on the road…" But Sihon refused. Numbers 21:23: "Sihon would not allow Israel to pass…" Instead, he gathered his army and came out to fight. Some battles you didn't start, but you still have to finish.

Numbers 21:24–25. Israel defeated Sihon. Took his land from Arnon to Jabbok. Arnon means "Roaring / rushing stream." Represents strong boundaries, transitions, crossing points. Jabbok means "Emptying / pouring out." Represents surrender, transformation, release. To take territory, you must cross boundaries and release what you were holding.

Heshbon, Sihon's capital, means "Reasoning / intelligence / calculation." This is powerful. The enemy was ruling from a place of calculated thinking. Some resistance is strategic, not emotional. It tries to outthink you, outmaneuver you, out plan you. For creatives: overthinking, analysis paralysis, trying to perfect instead of produce. You can't outthink obedience.

Scripture shows they had a strategy. They didn't just react. They advanced with direction. They moved with intention, alignment, divine timing.

Momentum is not movement; it is movement with direction. Momentum is movement sustained over time, movement with force and direction.

Joshua 1:7–8: "Be strong… do not turn… then you will have success…" Galatians 6:9: "Do not grow weary in doing good…" 1 Corinthians 15:58: "Be steadfast… always abounding…"

Resistance is sent to break your momentum. Because if momentum stops, progress stops, growth stops, possession is delayed.

For creatives: starting and stopping, inconsistency, losing rhythm. The enemy doesn't have to destroy you; he just has to disrupt your momentum.

This giant introduces conflict. Not all conflict is demonic, but all conflict must be handled correctly.

Romans 12:18: "As much as lies within you, live peaceably…" Matthew 5:9: "Blessed are the peacemakers…"

How to deal with conflict: Don't react, respond. Pause before responding. James 1:19: "Be quick to hear, slow to speak…" Don't respond emotionally. Respond intentionally. Reaction is emotional, response is strategic.

Say less, say right. Not every thought needs to be spoken. Be clear. Be direct. Be wise. Proverbs 15:1: "A soft answer turns away wrath…"

How to respond, practically: Don't assume tone. Don't escalate. Stay solution-focused. Ask: What is the goal? What is the outcome I want? You win more battles with wisdom than with volume.

For creatives, this shows up as creative differences, ego clashes, miscommunication, leadership tension. In rooms where ideas matter, expression matters, conflict can escalate quickly. You can be gifted and still mishandle conflict.

SIGNS YOU ARE DEALING WITH THE GIANT OF SIHON

Sihon was the king of the Amorites who refused to allow Israel passage through his territory (Numbers 21:21–24; Deuteronomy 2:24–37). Israel was not initially looking for a fight. They simply wanted to move forward. Yet Sihon came out against them and opposed their progress.

Spiritually, Sihon represents resistance, opposition, obstruction, unnecessary battles, territorial spirits, stubborn barriers, and anything that attempts to block God-ordained advancement.

Sihon is the giant that stands in the road. He is the giant that says "You can't go any further." "You'll never get there." "This door will remain closed." "This opportunity is not for you."

Unlike some giants that attack through fear or deception, Sihon attacks through resistance. His purpose is to stop movement. His purpose is to delay progress. His purpose is to make people abandon their journey.

You may be dealing with the giant of Sihon if:

- You repeatedly encounter unusual resistance.
- Progress seems constantly blocked.
- Doors that should open remain closed.
- Every step forward feels like a battle.
- You become discouraged by continual obstacles.
- You experience frustration from delays.
- You find yourself wanting to quit because of opposition.
- You feel stuck between where you are and where God promised you would be.
- You encounter repeated roadblocks despite doing the right things.
- You feel like you are constantly pushing uphill.
- You become weary from fighting the same battle repeatedly.
- You question whether the promise is worth pursuing.
- You feel delayed but not denied.

The giant of Sihon specializes in making people believe that resistance means they should stop.

HOW SIHON ATTACKS LEADERS

Leaders often encounter Sihon when they are approaching expansion. The giant whispers "The timing is wrong." "The resources aren't available." "The people won't support it." "This vision will never happen." "Just stay where you are."

Sihon attacks momentum. He attacks growth. He attacks movement. Many leaders mistakenly assume opposition means God is saying no.

Often opposition means they are moving in the right direction.

The giant of Sihon wants leaders to interpret resistance as rejection. He wants them to abandon assignments prematurely. He understands that many visions fail, not because they were impossible, but because people stopped pushing.

Leaders must learn that resistance is often part of advancement.

HOW SIHON ATTACKS CREATIVES

Creatives frequently encounter Sihon through obstacles and delays.

The giant whispers "You've waited too long." "The market is crowded." "Nobody is interested." "Give up." "It is not worth the effort."

As a result, creatives abandon projects just before breakthrough. Books stop at chapter ten. Businesses stop before launch. Songs remain unfinished. Ideas remain undeveloped.

The giant of Sihon understands that discouragement is often more effective than defeat. If he can convince creatives to stop themselves, he does not have to stop them.

Many creative dreams die because people interpret resistance as a sign to quit instead of a challenge to persevere.

PROPHETIC INSIGHT

One of the most remarkable things about Sihon is that Israel did not seek conflict with him. They sought passage. Yet God allowed the confrontation. Why? Because some territories cannot be possessed without confronting what is blocking access.

Many people pray for open doors while avoiding necessary battles. Some doors do not open automatically. Some doors open after opposition is confronted.

Prophetically, many believers are experiencing unusual resistance because they are approaching new territory. The resistance is not proof that God is absent. The resistance may be proof that something valuable is ahead. The enemy rarely fights people who are standing still. He fights people who are advancing.

This is a reminder that opposition is often confirmation, not cancellation. Do not confuse resistance with rejection. Do not confuse delays with denial. Do not confuse obstacles with impossibilities.

God is still leading. God is still opening doors. God is still making a way.

HOW TO CRUSH THE GIANT OF SIHON

Crushing Sihon begins by refusing to quit. Expect resistance. Do not be surprised by opposition. Maintain your focus on the promise rather than the obstacle.

Pray through delays. Persevere through setbacks. Develop endurance. Continue moving forward even when progress appears slow. Refuse to interpret every challenge as a closed door.

Seek God's wisdom during seasons of resistance. Strengthen your faith through Scripture. Remember previous victories. Most importantly, understand that persistence often breaks barriers that talent alone cannot overcome.

Keep moving forward. Don't stop because it got hard. Pressure is not permission to quit. Contend, don't avoid. Engage the battle. Some things only move when you confront them.

Follow God's timing. "Now begin to possess…" Timing matters.

Don't take it personal. It's about territory. You're not being attacked, you're being opposed. Protect your momentum. Stay consistent. Stay disciplined. Stay focused. Momentum is maintained through discipline.

Sihon represents resistance that tries to stop movement. But when you keep moving, resistance turns into reward. The giant of Sihon thrives when people quit. He loses when people keep moving.

PRAYER FOR CRUSHING THE GIANT OF SIHON

Father, in the name of Jesus, I come before You surrendering every frustration, delay, obstacle, and resistance that has attempted to discourage me. Lord, there have been moments when opposition made me question Your promises, but today I choose faith over frustration.

Strengthen me where I have become weary. Encourage me where I have become discouraged. Help me recognize the difference between a closed door and a challenge that requires perseverance.

Break every spirit of intimidation, discouragement, and hopelessness. Give me wisdom to navigate obstacles and courage to continue moving forward.

Lord, teach me not to quit when resistance appears. Help me trust Your timing, Your process, and Your plan. I declare that every barrier standing between me and my God-given purpose must yield to Your authority.

I receive fresh strength, fresh endurance, and fresh determination.

In Jesus' name, Amen.

DECLARATIONS FOR CRUSHING THE GIANT OF SIHON

- I refuse to quit.
- Opposition will not stop my progress.
- Resistance is not rejection.

- Delays are not denial.
- God is making a way for me.
- Every barrier must yield to God's purpose.
- I have the strength to endure.
- I will not grow weary in well-doing.
- I am advancing into my promised territory.
- Every obstacle is temporary.
- God's promises are still true.
- I move forward in faith.
- I refuse discouragement.
- I refuse defeat.
- The doors God opens cannot be closed by man.
- I am equipped for every challenge before me.
- Breakthrough belongs to me.
- I do not merely defeat giants, I crush them.

SPECIAL INSIGHT: THE GIANT OF RESISTANCE

One of the greatest lessons from Sihon is that not every battle is personal. Some battles are positional. Sihon opposed Israel because they were moving toward promise. Likewise, many believers become discouraged because they assume resistance means they are failing.

The opposite is often true. Resistance frequently appears when movement begins. When muscles grow, they encounter resistance. When leaders grow, they encounter resistance. When ministries grow, they encounter resistance. When businesses grow, they encounter resistance. When faith grows, it encounters resistance.

The presence of resistance does not mean God has abandoned the journey. Often it means the journey has become significant.

The giant of Sihon wants you to stop because the destination matters. Keep walking. Keep believing. Keep advancing. The promise is still ahead.

ISHBI-BENOB

The Fatigue/Weariness Giant

Scripture: 2 Samuel 21:15–17.

Meaning: "His dwelling is in Nob" / associated with high place, habitation.

Root: Fatigue, weariness, exhaustion (physical, emotional, spiritual).

Life Application: Burnout, mental exhaustion, lack of clarity due to fatigue, making decisions while drained. Goliath didn't show up at the beginning of David's journey. He showed up after years of battle. 2 Samuel 21:15: "David waxed faint…" David was tired. David was weary. David was depleted. And that's when the giant attacked. Rest strategically, stay covered (community).

CONTEXT

Fatigue is a doorway for attack.

The story reveals that David had already fought Goliath, led armies, won battles, and built influence. This was battle after battle after battle, and now here we are again, another war, another fight, another giant. This giant attacks those who have been consistently fighting. This is not for beginners. This is for seasoned warriors.

For creatives, you've been producing, you've been showing up, you've been carrying weight. Consistency without recovery leads to vulnerability. This giant does not strike when you are strong. It strikes when you are tired, overextended, emotionally drained, spiritually low. The enemy waits for your weakest moment, not your strongest.

The name Nob means "high place / place of priests." This is powerful. This giant is connected to calling, leadership, and responsibility. In Scripture, high places are consistently referenced as places of worship, sacrifice, and spiritual activity.

1 Kings 3:2 says, "The people sacrificed in high places." 2 Kings 17:10–11 says, "They set up high places… and burned incense…"

High places were often places of worship, places of encounter, and places of influence. But not all high places were godly. 2 Kings 23:13 shows that high places were also used for idolatry. High places amplify whatever is on them, whether it is God or something else.

High places represent influence, authority, and visibility. Matthew 4:8–9 shows that even Jesus was taken to a high place to be tempted.

High places are where promotion and temptation meet. The enemy targets high places because they affect more people, they shape environments, and they carry influence. If he can corrupt the high place, he can corrupt what flows from it.

High places are places of elevation, authority, and worship, but they are also places of exposure, pressure, and confrontation. The higher you go, the more visible you become, and the more you become a target.

High places are where influence increases, responsibility increases, and spiritual warfare increases. High places are not just places of promotion; they are places of testing. Because high places control influence, visibility, and impact, if the enemy can attack you there, he can affect everything connected to you. The attack is not just about you, it's about what flows through you.

Nob was not just any place. It was a priestly place. 1 Samuel 21:1 shows that Nob was where the priests served. In Scripture, priests represent those who minister to God, carry presence, and stand between God and people.

Priests were responsible for offering sacrifices. Leviticus 6:12–13 says, "The fire shall ever be burning upon the altar..." They maintained the fire, the altar, and the sacrifice. They kept the fire going. Priests also handled the Word. Malachi 2:7 says, "The priest's lips should keep knowledge..." They taught truth and communicated God's Word. They also stood between God and people.

Ezekiel 44:23 says, "They shall teach my people the difference..." They helped people discern, understand, and align. Priests didn't just serve God; they carried responsibility for people. If you are a leader, a creative, or a visionary, you function in a priestly capacity.

For creatives, you set atmosphere, you shape culture, and you influence hearts. 1 Peter 2:9 says, "You are a royal priesthood." You are not just creating, you are ministering. Creatives are modern-day carriers of atmosphere.

This giant targets priests because priests carry oil, carry responsibility, and carry weight. If the enemy can exhaust the priest, he can affect the people. If he can wear you out, he can weaken what flows through you.

Leviticus 10:1–2 shows that when priests were off, it affected everything. When the priest is weak, the system is affected. Fatigue at a high place is more dangerous than fatigue at a low place because more people are affected, more is at stake, and more is connected to you.

For creatives, when you're tired, your creativity suffers. When you're drained, your clarity suffers. When you're depleted, your influence weakens. You are not just managing your energy; you are stewarding your assignment.

Deuteronomy 12:2–3 shows that God instructed them to destroy wrong high places and rebuild correctly. High places must be maintained correctly or they become places of compromise.

Fatigue at a high place is dangerous because too much is connected to you. You are carrying influence, carrying responsibility, and carrying assignment. You are not just tired; you are under attack in a high place. The higher the calling, the greater the need for sustainability. For creatives, this includes leading teams, carrying vision, and producing under pressure.

But the story does not end there. In 2 Samuel 21:17, Abishai came to David's aid and struck the Philistine. Abishai, whose name means "my father is a gift," recognized that David was tired, stepped in without hesitation, fought when David could not, and protected the leader. This reveals that God will send people to cover you when you cannot cover yourself. The question becomes: who is your Abishai? Who sees when you are tired, steps in without being asked, and protects your capacity? If you do not have covering, you are exposed. For creatives, who helps carry your vision and guards your strength?

They told David, "You are the lamp of Israel." This is significant. You are not just a fighter; you are a light. For creatives, your work illuminates, your voice influences, and your gift impacts others. If you burn out, you dim what God called you to light.

This is why rest is not optional, it is strategy. In 1 Kings 19:5–8, Elijah was exhausted, and God did not rebuke him, God fed him. "Arise and eat, because the journey is too great for you." This reveals that you cannot eat for where you are; you must eat for where you are going. This is not just natural food, this is spiritual nourishment, renewal, and restoration. For creatives, you must refill, you must be poured into, and you must be strengthened. You cannot create from empty.

Scripture says Elijah slept, and God allowed it. Rest is not weakness, it is strategy. Fatigue made him vulnerable, but rest restored him. When Elijah opened his eyes, the provision was already there. This reveals that what you need is already present—fatigue just blinds you to it. For creatives, the ideas are there, the opportunities are there, and the resources are there, but exhaustion makes you miss it. Then the instruction came again: "Eat again." One moment of rest is not enough for a long journey. You need consistent renewal, consistent rest, and consistent filling.

The danger of fatigue is that it affects discernment, response, and clarity. You do not make your best decisions when you are tired. This is why this giant must be confronted strategically. You crush this giant by recognizing fatigue early, resting intentionally, staying covered, setting boundaries, and restoring your source. According to Matthew 11:28 and Isaiah 40:31, strength must be renewed, it is not automatic.

Fatigue is a strategic attack against your endurance. But you will not be taken out. You will not burn out. You will not be taken out by exhaustion. You will rest, you will recover, and you will be restored. Every attack that comes when you are weak will not succeed, because the journey ahead of you requires strength.

SIGNS YOU ARE DEALING WITH THE GIANT OF ISHBI-BENOB

Scripture: 2 Samuel 21:15-17

The story of Ishbi-Benob reveals a powerful truth. David had already defeated Goliath. He had already won battles. He had already established a kingdom. Yet one day, after years of fighting, Scripture says: "David waxed faint."

That phrase may be one of the most important warnings in the Bible. The giant of Ishbi-Benob does not wait until you are weak. He waits until you are weary. He waits until you are tired. He waits until you are depleted. He waits until you have been carrying responsibility for too long without replenishment.

This giant represents exhaustion, burnout, compassion fatigue, emotional depletion, spiritual weariness, decision fatigue, and vulnerability caused by prolonged warfare. You may be dealing with the giant of Ishbi-Benob if:

- You feel exhausted even after resting.
- You constantly feel overwhelmed.
- You have lost your passion.
- You struggle to enjoy things you once loved.
- You feel emotionally numb.
- You are increasingly irritable.
- Small problems feel enormous.
- You feel disconnected from God.
- You have little motivation.
- You feel physically, mentally, or emotionally drained.
- You have difficulty making decisions.
- You frequently think about quitting.
- You feel like you are running on empty.

- You struggle to recover from stress.
- You feel weary from carrying everyone else's burdens.

The giant of Ishbi-Benob thrives when people ignore their limitations.

HOW ISHBI-BENOB ATTACKS LEADERS

Leaders are one of this giant's favorite targets. David was a king when Ishbi-Benob attacked. This giant understands something many leaders forget: The higher the responsibility, the greater the need for replenishment. The giant whispers "You cannot stop." "Everyone needs you." "Keep pushing." "Take care of everyone else first." "Rest later."

Eventually leaders become depleted. They continue functioning externally while deteriorating internally. They preach tired. Lead tired. Serve tired. Counsel tired. Build tired. Love tired. Fight tired.

The giant of Ishbi-Benob understands that exhausted leaders often make decisions they would never make when healthy.

Many leadership failures begin long before the visible collapse. They begin with unaddressed fatigue. Burnout is often a giant disguised as dedication.

HOW ISHBI-BENOB ATTACKS CREATIVES

Creatives often encounter Ishbi-Benob after seasons of producing, creating, building, and serving. The giant whispers: "Keep creating." "Keep producing." "Keep giving." "Keep performing." "Keep posting." "Keep going."

Soon the creative becomes depleted. The well runs dry. Ideas stop flowing. Passion fades. Joy disappears. What once felt life-giving begins to feel exhausting.

The giant wants creatives to become machines instead of humans. It convinces them that their value comes from productivity. As a result, many gifted creatives burn out while trying to sustain unrealistic expectations. The giant of Ishbi-Benob does not fear your gift. It fears your sustainability.

PROPHETIC INSIGHT

One of the most powerful lessons in the story of Ishbi-Benob is that David did not defeat this giant alone. Abishai stepped in and helped him. This is significant. Some giants require community.

Many people have been taught that strength means doing everything alone. Scripture teaches something different. There are battles where God sends help. There are seasons where wisdom requires support. There are moments where strength looks like receiving assistance.

Prophetically, many people are carrying assignments that were never meant to be carried alone. The Lord is exposing unhealthy self-reliance. He is calling people into healthy support systems. Healthy relationships. Healthy boundaries. Healthy rhythms.

The giant of Ishbi-Benob often appears when people have confused being available with being assigned. Not every burden belongs to you. Not every emergency is your responsibility. Not every battle is yours to fight.

God is restoring balance to His people.

HOW TO CRUSH THE GIANT OF ISHBI-BENOB

Crushing Ishbi-Benob begins with recognizing your limitations. Rest is not weakness. Rest is wisdom. Create healthy boundaries. Protect your time. Protect your emotional health. Protect your spiritual health. Learn to say no. Learn to delegate. Learn to receive help.

Develop rhythms of recovery. Prioritize prayer. Prioritize Sabbath. Prioritize replenishment. Listen to your body. Listen to your emotions. Listen to the Holy Spirit. Most importantly, stop wearing exhaustion as a badge of honor. Burnout is not proof of faithfulness. Sustainability is. God did not design you merely to survive. He designed you to endure.

PRAYER FOR CRUSHING THE GIANT OF ISHBI-BENOB

Father, in the name of Jesus, I bring before You every area of exhaustion, fatigue, burnout, weariness, and depletion in my life. Lord, you know every battle I have fought, every burden I have carried, and every responsibility I have attempted to manage.

Today I surrender my weariness to You.

Forgive me for every time I tried to carry burdens You never assigned to me. Forgive me for every time I ignored my need for rest, replenishment, and recovery.

Lord, renew my strength. Restore my joy. Refresh my spirit. Heal every area of emotional, mental, physical, and spiritual exhaustion.

Teach me healthy boundaries. Teach me healthy rhythms. Teach me when to work and when to rest.

Send the right people into my life to support, strengthen, and encourage me.

I reject burnout. I reject exhaustion. I reject unhealthy striving. I receive Your peace. I receive Your strength. I receive Your renewal. In Jesus' name, Amen.

DECLARATIONS

- My strength comes from the Lord.
- I will not be consumed by exhaustion.
- God is renewing my strength daily.
- I reject burnout and embrace balance.
- Rest is part of God's plan for my life.
- I am not required to carry every burden.
- God is teaching me healthy boundaries.
- I receive wisdom for every assignment.
- My joy is being restored.
- My passion is being renewed.
- I am refreshed mentally, emotionally, physically, and spiritually.
- God is surrounding me with healthy support.
- I refuse unhealthy striving.
- I choose sustainability over burnout.
- I choose wisdom over overwork.
- I am strong in the Lord and in the power of His might.
- I will finish my assignment with strength.
- I do not merely defeat giants, I crush them.

SPECIAL INSIGHT: THE DANGER OF WEARY WARRIORS

Many people prepare for attack when they are weak. Few prepare for attack when they are weary. Yet Scripture says David's danger came when he became faint. Not sinful. Not rebellious. Not fearful. Just tired.

This is why the enemy often targets pastors, caregivers, counselors, therapists, creatives, parents, entrepreneurs, and leaders. These are people who spend much of their lives pouring into others.

The giant of Ishbi-Benob understands that exhausted people often lose perspective. They begin making permanent decisions based on temporary fatigue. What feels impossible today may simply require rest. Sometimes you do not need a new calling. You need recovery. Sometimes you do not need a new strategy. You need replenishment. Sometimes you do not need to quit. You need sleep. A weary warrior is vulnerable. A renewed warrior is dangerous.

The giant of Ishbi-Benob falls when God's people learn that rest is not the enemy of productivity. It is the fuel for it.

SAPH

The Threshold / Transition Giant

Scripture: 2 Samuel 21:18; 1 Chronicles 20:4.

Meaning: Threshold / doorway / edge.

Saph appears during a continued series of battles. "After this there was again a battle…" This is important. This was not the first fight. This was not the last fight. This was a battle in a new phase. Victory in one season does not eliminate battles in the next. You can win yesterday and still have to fight today. For creatives, you finish one assignment and another demand shows up. New levels come with new fights.

The Root of this giant is transition, movement between levels, and resistance at entry points.

In life application, this looks like stepping into something new, shifting into a new identity, entering new territory, and becoming who God called you to be.

This giant doesn't fight where you've been, it fights where you're going. Transition is not just about crossing over. It is not just about leaving one place and getting to another. Transition is about what happens in between.

Trans means across, beyond, from one place to another. Sit represents process, posture, peace, rest, and preparation. Ion represents state, condition, and ongoing process.

Transition is not just where you are going, it is what you do in the sit on the way there. Transition is not just movement. It is movement with formation. It is movement with preparation. It is movement with becoming. The sit is the part most people want to skip, but it is in the sit that your character is formed, your thinking is corrected, your weight is shifted, your responsibility is developed, your peace is tested, and your rest is learned. It is what you do in the sit that prepares you for the other side of the transition. The sit is not laziness, delay, or stagnation. The sit is where God works on you.

Transition is not just about pace. It is also about peace. It is also about rest. If you move without peace, you arrive unstable. If you move without rest, you arrive without strength to sustain it. Perfect peace comes from a stayed mind. God gives rest in His presence. There remains a rest for God's people. God's peace and God's rest are part of transition.

The "ion" speaks to process. Transition is not a moment. It is a condition of becoming. Transition picks up the person you are and carries you toward the person you must become. God is not just changing your location; He is changing you. He is teaching you how to carry more, how to handle more, and how to sustain more. You don't arrive first, you become first.

In Judges 19:26–27, the woman came to the door and her hands were on the threshold. She had endured trauma, abuse, and exhaustion. She made it to the door, but she collapsed at the threshold. You can survive the journey and still collapse at the door. She was right there. Help was on the other side. The door was within reach, but she didn't cross. Don't collapse where you are called to cross. You are too close to quit. You are too close to stop. What's on the other side is promise, purpose, and fulfillment. The threshold is not your resting place; it is your crossing place.

Saph means threshold, doorway, or edge. It is the space between past and future, old and new, identity and assignment. The greatest resistance happens at the point of entry. This giant shows up because thresholds represent access, movement, and possession. If the enemy can stop you here, he can stop everything connected to you.

This giant fights your crossing, not your calling. This shows up as hesitation, delay, second-guessing, and fear of finishing. You're right there, but something holds you back.

For creatives, this looks like creating but not releasing, building but not launching, and preparing but not stepping out. Many creatives don't fail; they stall at the threshold.

Sibbecai struck Saph. His name means "The Lord has intervened." God will send help at the threshold. You are not alone at the door.

To crush this giant, you must move. Movement breaks hesitation. You cannot stay at the door. Silence overthinking. Stop analyzing and start moving. Overthinking kills transition. Finish, because completion is warfare. What you finish unlocks what's next. Trust God. Push through.

Expect resistance. Resistance means you are close. The threshold is not where you stop, it is where you cross. I will not collapse at the door. I will not stop at the edge. I will move. I will finish. I will cross. Everything waiting on the other side, I will possess. You are not just crossing over, you are becoming.

SIGNS YOU ARE DEALING WITH THE GIANT OF SAPH

Scripture: 2 Samuel 21:18; 1 Chronicles 20:4

Saph was one of the remaining descendants of the giants defeated during David's reign. While Goliath often receives the attention, Saph reveals another important truth about giants. Sometimes after a major victory, another giant appears. Sometimes after one battle ends, another begins. Sometimes after breakthrough, another challenge emerges.

Spiritually, the giant of Saph represents threshold battles, recurring opposition, unfinished warfare, spiritual transitions, and resistance that appears at the doorway of a new season.

Saph is the giant of "almost." Almost free. Almost healed. Almost promoted. Almost through. Almost there. The giant appears at critical transition points. Its assignment is to stop people from crossing into the next season of their lives.

You may be dealing with the giant of Saph if:

- You repeatedly encounter obstacles when approaching breakthrough.
- You experience unusual resistance during transitions.
- Things seem to fall apart just before success.
- You often feel like you're making progress only to encounter new opposition.
- You struggle to finish what you start.
- You become discouraged near the end of a process.
- You notice recurring battles at key moments of advancement.
- You frequently feel stuck between seasons.
- You battle frustration after significant victories.
- You find yourself asking, "Why is this happening now?"
- You feel opposition intensify when you're close to breakthrough.

- You are tempted to quit just before completion.
- You experience repeated resistance around major decisions.

The giant of Saph thrives at thresholds. It wants people to retreat when they are closest to crossing over.

HOW SAPH ATTACKS LEADERS

Leaders often encounter Saph during seasons of growth, transition, and expansion. Saph attacks leaders when they are moving from one level of influence to another. From small to large. From local to regional. From vision to implementation. From survival to expansion.

The giant understands that transitions create vulnerability. It attempts to convince leaders that discomfort means danger. As a result, leaders may sabotage growth because the next level feels unfamiliar. Many leaders do not lose because they lack ability. They lose because they retreat at the threshold.

HOW SAPH ATTACKS CREATIVES

Creatives frequently encounter Saph when they are close to releasing something significant. As a result, projects remain trapped in perpetual development. Creative people often mistake hesitation for wisdom. The giant of Saph thrives in delay. Its goal is not always to destroy the dream. Its goal is to postpone it indefinitely. Many creatives are not defeated by failure. They are defeated by endless postponement.

PROPHETIC INSIGHT

One of the most powerful truths about Saph is that he appeared after previous giants had already been defeated. This teaches us that breakthrough is not always a single event. It is often a process. The enemy hopes people will become discouraged when another battle appears. He wants them to believe that because another giant emerged, the previous victories did not matter. But every victory matters. Every breakthrough matters. Every healed wound matters. Every lesson matters. Prophetically, many people are standing at the edge of a new season. A new ministry. A new business. A new assignment. A new relationship. A new level of healing.

The enemy is attempting to create discouragement at the threshold. Do not confuse transition with trouble. Do not confuse resistance with rejection. Do not confuse discomfort with danger. You are closer than you think.

Many people are fighting because they are approaching breakthrough, not because they are moving away from it.

HOW TO CRUSH THE GIANT OF SAPH

Crushing Saph begins by refusing to quit near the finish line. Recognize that transition often creates pressure. Expect opposition during seasons of growth. Finish what God started in you. Keep moving forward. Trust God's timing. Refuse discouragement. Celebrate progress instead of focusing only on what remains.

Maintain momentum. Stay connected to God's promises. Seek wise counsel during seasons of transition. Most importantly, remember that the pressure often increases because the breakthrough is near. The giant of Saph wants you to stop at the doorway. God wants you to walk through it.

PRAYER FOR CRUSHING THE GIANT OF SAPH

Father, in the name of Jesus, I thank You for every victory You have already brought into my life. Today I surrender every fear, frustration, delay, and discouragement that has attempted to stop me from entering the next season You have prepared for me.

Lord, strengthen me at every threshold. Give me courage when transitions feel uncomfortable. Help me trust you when new seasons require new levels of faith.

Break every spirit of delay, hesitation, intimidation, and discouragement. Remove every obstacle that seeks to prevent me from crossing into my God-given future.

Teach me to persevere. Teach me to endure. Teach me to finish what You have called me to complete. I declare that I will not retreat at the doorway of breakthrough. I will move forward in faith, confidence, and obedience.

In Jesus' name, Amen.

DECLARATIONS FOR CRUSHING THE GIANT OF SAPH

- I will not quit at the threshold.
- I am moving into my next season.
- God is leading me forward.
- I refuse delay and discouragement.
- Resistance will not stop my progress.
- I will finish what God has called me to do.
- Every transition is preparing me for greater purpose.
- I trust God's timing.
- I trust God's process.
- I am equipped for the next level.
- I will not retreat because of discomfort.
- My breakthrough is closer than I realize.
- I walk boldly through every open door.
- Fear will not keep me from advancement.
- God is completing the work He began in me.

- I possess every promise God has spoken.
- The threshold belongs to me.
- I do not merely defeat giants, I crush them.

SPECIAL INSIGHT: THE GIANT OF THE THRESHOLD

One of the enemy's most effective strategies is discouraging people near completion. The Israelites experienced this repeatedly. So did David. So did many of God's servants throughout Scripture. Why? Because the enemy understands something important: A person who never starts can be discouraged. But a person who is almost finished is dangerous.

The giant of Saph appears near transitions because transitions create momentum. New levels create influence. New territory creates impact. New seasons create growth. The enemy cannot change God's promise. But he will attempt to make people abandon it.

Do not let temporary resistance make you abandon permanent promises. The pressure may be increasing because you are standing at the threshold. Do not stop now. Cross over. Walk through. Keep moving.

The giant standing at the doorway is often proof that something valuable is on the other side. Remember one of the core truths of Crushing the Giants:

A giant is not a sign to run. A giant is an announcement that you are standing near promise.

And Saph is often the announcement that you're standing at the door.

LAHMI

The Provision/Supply Giant

Scripture: 1 Chronicles 20:5; 2 Samuel 21:19.

Meaning: "My bread" / sustenance / provision. "…Elhanan… killed Lahmi the brother of Goliath…"

This is important. Lahmi is connected to Goliath. Some giants are connected. You defeat one and another connected to it shows up. What you don't fully deal with will reappear in another form.

The root of this giant is provision, supply, sustenance, and financial flow. In life application, this shows up as lack of resources, inconsistent income, fear of not having enough, and difficulty sustaining what God started.

This giant doesn't fight your calling; it fights your ability to sustain it.

CONTEXT

Lahmi means "my bread." Bread represents daily provision, supply, and what sustains you. "Give us this day our daily bread…"

This giant targets your daily flow, not just big moments, but consistency, sustainability, and ongoing provision. This giant attacks income, opportunities, stability, and structure. It wants you to start but not sustain, build but not maintain, and receive but not manage. It's not enough to start, you must sustain.

For creatives, this shows up as inconsistent money, undervaluing your work, lack of structure, and creating without monetizing. You're gifted but not sustained. Many creatives don't lack talent; they lack structure and stewardship.

Lahmi is the brother of Goliath. Intimidation and lack are connected. If the enemy can intimidate you, he can control your provision. You won't charge what you're worth, step into opportunity, or expand your capacity. Fear will shrink your value.

Elhanan killed Lahmi. His name means "God has been gracious." Provision is connected to grace. You are not sustaining yourself alone. What God gives grace for, He provides for.

Before you defeat this giant, you must understand money. Many people don't have a money problem; they have a relationship problem with money. If your relationship with money is wrong, your

results will be wrong.

Money is a tool, a resource, and a system of exchange. Money is not your source, your identity, or your security. "The love of money is the root..." Money is a tool; God is your source.

"My people are destroyed for lack of knowledge..." Not lack of money, but lack of understanding. Money does not respond to need; it responds to stewardship.

Philippians 4:15–17 teaches partnership, not just giving. "No church communicated with me as concerning giving and receiving..." "...Not because I desire a gift: but I desire fruit that may abound to your account." Giving is not about what God needs, it's about what is released to you.

Giving is tied to your account. There are record, fruit, and return. When you give, something is credited to your account. Giving produces something. "But my God shall supply all your need..." This is connected to giving, sowing, and partnership.

Provision follows participation. "For God so loved... that He gave..." Giving is the expression of love and the pathway to increase. "Give, and it shall be given..." "He who sows..." "Bring the tithe..." "The generous soul shall be made rich..." Generosity breaks the back of lack.

Many creatives struggle here because income fluctuates, fear increases, and a scarcity mindset develops. So, they hold on. Closed hands stop flow. When you give, you activate flow. You cannot expect overflow with closed hands. When you give, you partner, you position, and you participate. Then God supplies.

SIGNS YOU ARE DEALING WITH THE GIANT OF LAHMI

Scripture: 1 Chronicles 20:5

Lahmi was the brother of Goliath and one of the descendants of the giants. While Goliath often represents intimidation, Lahmi reveals something deeper. The name Lahmi is connected to the Hebrew word for bread and provision. For that reason, within the Crushing the Giants framework, Lahmi represents lack, scarcity, financial pressure, resource shortages, poverty thinking, limitation, and the fear of not having enough.

The giant of Lahmi constantly asks "What if there isn't enough?" "What if you run out?" "What if God doesn't provide?" "What if you can't afford it?" Lahmi is not always about actual poverty. Often it is about a poverty mindset. A person can have resources and still think like they have none. The giant thrives on fear of lack.

You may be dealing with the giant of Lahmi if:

- You constantly worry about money.
- You struggle to trust God as your provider.
- You operate from scarcity rather than abundance.
- You hoard because you fear running out.
- You avoid opportunities because of financial fear.
- You constantly focus on what you lack.
- You feel limited by resources.
- You struggle with generosity.
- You frequently say, "I can't afford it," before seeking God's wisdom.
- You believe there is never enough time, money, opportunity, or support.
- You become anxious whenever resources decrease.
- You compare your resources to other people's resources.
- You expect lack more than provision.
- You live with a constant fear of insufficiency.

The giant of Lahmi attempts to make people trust their resources more than they trust God.

HOW LAHMI ATTACKS LEADERS

Leaders frequently encounter Lahmi when God gives them a vision larger than their budget. Lahmi attempts to make leaders shrink the vision to fit the resources instead of trusting God to expand the resources to fit the vision. Many ministries, organizations, and businesses die because leaders become consumed by limitations.

The giant wants leaders to focus on what is missing rather than what God has already provided. It creates fear-based leadership. It creates survival-based decision-making. It causes leaders to think small when

God is thinking large. The giant of Lahmi knows that scarcity thinking can cripple even the greatest vision.

HOW LAHMI ATTACKS CREATIVES

Creatives often encounter Lahmi through financial fear and resource limitations. The giant whispers "You can't afford to start." "You don't have the right equipment." "You don't have enough support." "You don't have enough followers." "You don't have enough connections." As a result, creatives postpone their dreams. The giant of Lahmi convinces creatives that they need perfect resources before they can begin. But throughout Scripture, God repeatedly used people who started with very little.

The giant is not afraid of what you have. It is afraid of what God can multiply.

PROPHETIC INSIGHT

One of the greatest lessons throughout Scripture is that God rarely begins with abundance. He often begins with insufficiency. A widow had a little oil. A boy had a small lunch. Moses had a rod. David had a sling. The disciples had a few fish and loaves. Again and again, God demonstrated that provision is not determined by quantity. It is determined by His blessing.

The giant of Lahmi wants people to believe that resources create possibility. God teaches that obedience creates possibility.

Prophetically, many people have delayed assignments because they feel under-resourced. The Lord is reminding them that He is not limited by what they lack. He is able to provide what is needed at the proper time. Many people are waiting for provision before they obey.

Often provision follows obedience. God is still Jehovah Jireh. The Lord who provided then still provides now.

HOW TO CRUSH THE GIANT OF LAHMI

Crushing Lahmi begins by renewing your perspective on provision. Stop focusing exclusively on what is missing. Start recognizing what God has already provided. Practice gratitude. Develop generosity. Trust God with your resources. Steward what you have faithfully. Take steps of obedience. Refuse fear-based decisions. Replace scarcity thinking with kingdom thinking.

Study God's promises regarding provision. Remember previous seasons where God provided. Most importantly, understand that provision is not merely financial. God provides wisdom. God provides favor. God provides relationships. God provides opportunities. God provides strength. The giant of Lahmi falls when trust replaces fear.

To crush this giant, renew your mind. Value your gift. Build structure. Steward well. Create consistency. Provision is not just what comes to you, it is what flows through you. You are not just called to start; you are called to sustain.

PRAYER FOR CRUSHING THE GIANT OF LAHMI

Father, in the name of Jesus, I thank You for being Jehovah Jireh, my Provider. Today I surrender every fear of lack, every anxiety about resources, and every scarcity mindset that has attempted to influence my life.

Forgive me for every time I focused more on what I lacked than on Your faithfulness. Forgive me for trusting circumstances more than I trusted you.

Lord, renew my mind concerning provision. Help me see opportunities where I once saw obstacles. Help me see resources where I once saw limitations.

Break every spirit of fear, scarcity, poverty thinking, and financial anxiety. Teach me to steward wisely, give generously, and trust You completely.

I declare that You are my source. My confidence is not in money, people, systems, or circumstances. My confidence is in You.

Thank You for supplying every need according to Your riches in glory.

In Jesus' name, Amen.

DECLARATIONS

- God is my Provider.
- I refuse to live in fear of lack.
- I trust God's provision.
- Scarcity will not control my decisions.
- God supplies all my needs.
- I have more than enough for every assignment God gives me.
- I am a wise steward.
- I walk in faith and not fear.
- I reject poverty thinking.
- I embrace kingdom abundance.
- God's provision is not limited by my circumstances.
- Favor is surrounding me.
- Opportunities are opening before me.
- Resources are coming into alignment.
- I will not shrink my vision because of temporary limitations.
- God is multiplying what He has placed in my hands.
- I am blessed to be a blessing.

• I do not merely defeat giants, I crush them.

SPECIAL INSIGHT: POVERTY AND POVERTY THINKING ARE NOT THE SAME

One of the greatest deceptions of Lahmi is convincing people that poverty is only financial. Poverty often begins as a mindset. A person can have little and still think abundantly. A person can have much and still think fearfully.

Poverty thinking says "There will never be enough." "Someone else will get the opportunity." "I have to hold on to everything." "Resources are limited."

Kingdom thinking says "My source is God." "There is enough for my assignment." "What God has for me cannot be stolen by someone else." "Provision follows obedience."

The giant of Lahmi is ultimately not fighting your finances. It is fighting your trust. Because once people trust God as Provider, fear begins to lose its power. And when fear loses its power, the giant of Lahmi begins to fall.

CONCLUSION

The Giants Fell, But the Promise Remains

As we come to the end of this volume, one truth should be clearer than ever: God never intended for His people to live intimidated by giants.

From Genesis to Revelation, we see a God who continually calls ordinary people into extraordinary places. He calls them beyond their comfort zones, beyond their limitations, beyond their fears, and beyond what seems possible. Yet almost every time God prepared His people for advancement, there was opposition waiting. There were giants in the land. There were obstacles to overcome, battles to fight, territories to possess, and promises that required courage.

Throughout this volume, we have examined some of the named giants of Scripture. We have explored where they lived, what their names meant, how they operated, and how they stood between God's people and their inheritance. We have seen giants of intimidation, giants of fatigue, giants of comparison, giants of resistance, giants of strongholds, and giants that represented barriers to purpose, destiny, and promise.

Yet one consistent pattern emerged. The giant never had the final word. The giant was never greater than God's promise. The giant was never stronger than God's purpose. The giant was never larger than God's plan. Again and again, Scripture reminds us that giants may occupy the territory, but they do not own it. The promise belongs to God's people.

That truth is just as relevant today as it was thousands of years ago. You may not face an Anakim, a Rephaim, an Emim, a Zamzummim, or a Goliath in the natural. But you will face moments that seem larger than you. You will encounter obstacles that challenge your faith. You will face seasons where intimidation tries to silence you, fatigue tries to stop you, fear tries to paralyze you, and resistance tries to convince you to quit.

In those moments, remember what these giants taught us. The presence of a giant does not mean God has abandoned you. The presence of a giant does not mean you have missed your assignment. The presence of a giant does not mean the promise is unattainable. Often, the giant is evidence that you are standing at the edge of something significant. The giant is frequently an announcement that there is territory worth possessing. The giant reveals that there is purpose worth pursuing. The giant exposes that there is inheritance on the other side.

Many people spend their lives trying to avoid giants, but those who fulfill God's purpose learn to confront them. The men and women we celebrate throughout Scripture were not people who never encountered opposition; they were people who refused to surrender to it. Joshua faced giants. Caleb faced giants. David faced giants. The apostles faced giants. The early church faced giants. Yet they continued moving forward because they understood something powerful: victory does not belong to those who never face resistance. Victory belongs to those who refuse to stop moving when resistance appears.

Perhaps the greatest lesson from this volume is that every giant ultimately points us back to God. Giants reveal our dependence on Him. Giants expose the limits of our own strength. Giants teach us to trust His voice above the voices of fear. Giants remind us that the battle belongs to the Lord. And when the battle belongs to the Lord, the outcome is never determined by the size of the opposition. It is determined by the greatness of the God who fights for us.

As you close this book, do not simply remember the giants. Remember the victories. Remember the promises. Remember the faithfulness of God. Remember that every giant in Scripture eventually encountered someone who was willing to believe God more than they believed their fear.

Most importantly, remember that you were not created to merely survive the land. You were called to possess it. You were not called to spend your life staring at giants. You were called to move forward in faith. You were not called to live intimidated by opposition. You were called to advance despite it.

The giants may have occupied the land, but they were never the rightful owners of it. God's people were. And God's promise still stands today.

So, stand up. Move forward. Take courage. Possess the territory. Confront what stands in front of you. Crush what seeks to stop you.

And never forget: a giant is not a sign to retreat. A giant is an announcement that there is something worth possessing on the other side.

The giants have fallen. Their names may be remembered in Scripture, but their power was temporary, while God's promises remain eternal. Every giant that once seemed invincible eventually became a testimony of God's faithfulness and the courage of those who trusted Him. The same God who empowered Joshua, Caleb, David, and countless others is still at work today, calling His people to walk forward in faith rather than shrink back in fear. The story has never been about the size of the giant; it has always been about the greatness of God and His unwavering commitment to fulfill what He has promised.

Long after the giants were gone, the promise remained. Long after the battle ended, God's word still stood. Long after the opposition disappeared, the inheritance was still waiting to be possessed. The giants were never the destination. They were simply the resistance standing between God's people and what He had already determined to give them. In the same way, the battles you face today are not greater than God's purpose for your life. They are simply opportunities for His faithfulness to be revealed and His promises to be fulfilled.

Now go possess the promise.

Dr. Renetta S. Watson is an author, educator, and transformational leader

with over 35 years in ministry, 26 years in leadership, and more than two decades equipping, preaching, and teaching across diverse communities. Known as "The Equipper," Dr. Watson carries a calling rooted in Ephesians 4 equipping leaders to walk in purpose, maturity, and Kingdom effectiveness. Her life focus and mandate are to impact communities, influence culture, and invoke lasting change. Equipper is not a title or brand, but a divine calling and mission.

Dr. Watson is also a Nationally Certified Christian Counselor, Church Consultant, and Christian Life Coach. In addition to her ministry work, Dr. Watson spent several years teaching high school mathematics and behavior specialist working with students in the juvenile justice system.

Deeply committed to community transformation, Dr. Watson has served as a mentor, youth advocate, and community leader. She is the founder of EDUKATE Ministries, Equip Enterprises and Diamonds & Pearls Ministry.

Dr. Watson is also the author of Encouragement in the Storm, Developing Your Prayer Print, REAL8: Eight Principles for Healthy Relationships. The DREAM: A Blue Print for Evangelism & Discipleship, SOAR: Strategies for Creating Systems that Build Healthy Churches, and Ministry: The Call You Can't Decline. She is co-author of Diamonds and Pearls: The Crown & Covenant.

www.CrushingTheGiants.com

Made in the USA
Monee, IL
01 September 2026

60408267R00116